Oriental Carpets

A buyer's guide

Oriental Carpets

A buyer's guide

ESSIE SAKHAI

MOYER BELL

Wakefield, Rhode Island & London

Published by Moyer Bell

Copyright © by Essie Sakhai

LIBRARY OF CONGRESS
CATALOGING IN PUBLICATION DATA

Sakhai, Essie   Oriental carpets: a buyer's guide

1.Rugs, Oriental—Collectors and collecting.
I.Title.

NK2808.S27   1995   95-48424
746.7'5'095075—dc20   CIP

ISBN 1-55921-146-6

Printed in the United Kingdom
Distributed in North America by
Publishers Group West, P.O. Box 8843,
Emeryville CA 94662, 800–788–3123
(in California 510–658–3453)

Many people have helped in the making of this book.

I would particularly like to thank my father, Benny Sakhai, who inspired and encouraged my love of carpets. Most of my knowledge of these wonderful works of art comes from him. He is the best teacher I know.

I would also like to thank Arsalan Jaff, for all his assistance, Jinny Johnson for editing the text, Dave Goodman for designing the book and Caroline Sheard for compiling the index.

Essie Sakhai

For more information on the carpets illustrated in this book contact:

Essie Carpets
62 Piccadilly, London W1V 9HL
Telephone 0171 493 7766
Fax 0171 495 3456

or write to
·PO Box 2242, London NW8 7SF

Half title: A dazzling display of oriental carpets in the Blue Mosque, Istanbul, Turkey.

Title page: A detail from a Caucasian Shirvan multi-medallion design (*see* page 70-71).

Picture credits
Half title: Michael Jenner/Robert Harding Picture Library; *Page 19:* Adam Woolfitt/Robert Harding Picture Library; all other pictures supplied by Essie Sakhai

Artwork credits
Map and line drawings by Technical Art Services

Contents

ORIGINS

❧

If history is the written record of past events, then the tradition of carpet weaving is older than history itself. Carpets predate such written records and there is no proof as to exactly where and when the first carpets were made. Academics and experts champion their particular theories, but it is unlikely that the whole story of the development of this unique craft will ever be known.

One theory suggests that the first carpets were created by Central Asian nomads, who were unwilling to sacrifice valuable livestock simply to use their hides as floor coverings. However, these itinerant tent dwellers would still have needed rugs for comfort and warmth, and some experts believe that they may have devised a system of looping and knotting woollen threads into a shaggy pile that imitated animal pelts. Opponents of this theory claim that the nomads' lifestyle was too harsh and arduous to allow time for such creative innovation. Such a finely artistic craft as carpet making, they argue, could only have developed in the peace and order of a prosperous settled community.

However carpets began, it seems certain that the earliest examples would have been plain and unadorned. The urge to ornament would have come gradually, once the mechanics of the weaving process became fully understood. Even so, ancient cave paintings demonstrate that early humans quickly learned to explore their creative talents, and the earliest carpet designs may have featured stylized scenes of hunting and animals, similar to those seen in cave paintings.

The earliest, albeit oblique, references to carpets appear in the Old Testament and the writings of classical authors such as Homer and Aeschylus. There is no way of knowing exactly what kind of textiles these writings refer to. They may have been knotted carpets, but equally they could have been felted, woven or embroidered materials. One thing is sure, however—even at this time, such textiles were held in high esteem. In his play *Agamemnon*, Aeschylus relates how Clytemnestra spreads fine carpets at the feet of her homecoming husband. He is unwilling to walk on them, since that is an honour meant only for the gods, but is finally persuaded to do so.

> *Great the extravagance, and great the shame I feel*
> *to spoil such treasure and such silver's worth of webs.*

Aeschylus wrote these lines in about 500 BC, and the earliest real piece of evidence in the history of weaving, the Pazyryk carpet, is thought to date from that same time.

This carpet was discovered in 1949 in a royal burial mound in the Pazyryk mountains of Siberia. It had lain there for more than two thousand years, preserved by a thick layer of perma-frost. Archaeologists believe that the tomb was plundered by grave robbers shortly after it was originally sealed. Most of the valuable possessions left to ensure the royal occupant's comfortable passage into the next life were taken, but the carpet, which may have been thought too distinctive to sell or too large to carry, was left behind. It is ironic that it may have been the robbers' vandalism—the opening of the tomb allowed water to seep in that then froze to perma-frost—which caused the carpet to be preserved until the present day.

The Pazyryk carpet is incredible not only for its age but also for its craftsmanship. It is worked in a style of knot which is still used today and, with more than two hundred knots in every 2.5 square centimetres (1 square inch) of pile, its design has a delicacy which suggests its creation by craftsmen with a long tradition of weaving behind them. How long that tradition was will probably never be known, but it is certain that many more such ancient pieces must have existed and rotted away over the centuries.

One such vanished treasure was the Spring Carpet of Chosroes. According to legend, this carpet was woven in the middle of the first century AD to celebrate the defeat of the Romans and the conquest of southern Arabia by the Persian king, Chosroes I. Laden with designs worked in precious stones and gold thread, this massive memento weighed several tonnes and measured 122 metres long by 30 metres wide (400 x 100 feet). Over it ran "paths" along which, legend has it, Chosroes would wander, admiring the scene. Unfortunately for posterity, the king's subjects appear to have been better at weaving than they were at defending their newly won territories and in AD 641 the Persians were defeated by Arab invaders. The beautiful garden carpet was divided up by the victors and no part of it now survives.

A variety of carpets and fragments of carpets, dating from as early as the fifth century, have been found throughout the Middle East, proving that by this time the art of carpet weaving was widely practised. At the advent of Islam in the seventh century, carpet weaving had almost certainly been in existence for at least two thousand years. From this point on, the Islamic religion and the art of weaving developed side by side.

Invading armies and travelling traders helped spread both the carpet-making craft and the Islamic faith throughout the Near East and Central Asia. As large parts of this once troubled area were converted to Islam and its people settled under more centralized control, the energy which had once been put into territorial advances could be directed toward artistic and social achievements. A brilliant period of Islamic art began with the rise to power of the Seljuks, a Turkic people from Central Asia, in the twelfth and thirteenth centuries. Under court patronage, a distinct Islamic artistic style developed and the finest artists were commissioned to apply their designs to carpets.

In Persia, now generally considered the centre of fine carpet making, the art reached perhaps its highest form in the reign of the Safavid dynasty, which ruled the area during the sixteenth and seventeenth centuries. In this so-called Golden Era of Safavid patronage, the religious ban on the representation of living creatures was overturned and for the first time carpets were filled with depictions of birds and beasts. In line with the new realism, existing geometric patterns were gradually refined into the flowing arabesques and curlicues that are still part of the finest designs today.

One of the most famous of all Persian carpets, the Ardebil, dates from this period. The Ardebil carpet is one of a pair which came to England in extremely poor condition in 1893. One carpet was used to restore the other and, although the ethics of this decision are questioned by some, the Ardebil, now in the Victoria & Albert Museum in London, is a stunning example of just how glittering the work of the Golden Era was.

Court carpets attained new artistic heights, but weaving also continued to thrive as a genuine home craft. In nomadic tribes, country villages and town houses, the women of the family would weave whenever there was a moment spare from the domestic rituals. The designs they worked and the colours they used were learned from their mothers and grandmothers, and the carpets they made provided furnishing and ornament for the family home. When all their domestic needs had been met, the women continued to weave. These additional carpets became a kind of savings account, a reserve which could be sold off in times of financial need.

In short, carpets were a daily fact of life for everyone in Persia at that time. Royal families and the very wealthy had their own weaving workshops, while all but the poorest peasants had a rough-hewn loom set up in the yard or family room. The technical and artistic quality of their output might vary, but in all sectors of society carpets fulfilled much the same functions. As well as furnishings and ornaments, carpets were a form of currency so readily accepted that they could be used to pay for a daughter's dowry, buy extra sheep or even pay off taxes. To this day, the Iranian Inland Revenue is willing to take payment in carpets since they are so easily sold and keep their value.

During the Safavid dynasty, weaving was probably more highly regarded in Persia than in any other country, but the tradition was still strong elsewhere. In Turkey, rug weaving was traditionally an occupation for rural peasants, who made somewhat coarsely woven pieces with angular designs in bold colours. The carpets they produced were different in character from Persian carpets, not only for reasons of skill or even nationality but also because Turkish weavers still obeyed the old religious edict forbidding the representation of living creatures. In Turkish carpets, geometric patterns and stylized trees and flowers replaced the naturalistic birds and animals of Persian designs.

Closely related to the Turks are the Turkoman and Caucasian peoples of Central Asia who, some believe, may have actually invented the craft of weaving. Whether or not this is true, carpets certainly played a huge part in the lives of the descendants of these largely nomadic peoples. For them, as for so many carpet-weaving nations, carpets equalled wealth. To these nomads, that wealth was particularly valuable since it could be created on small portable looms from the simplest assets—wool, talent and time. Most of the rugs the tribes produced were put to domestic use as floor coverings, bags and even horse blankets. The surplus was sold in market towns, which frequently gave their names to the rugs traded there, regardless of the actual geographical origins of the items.

The tradition of Chinese carpet weaving has an entirely different background even though weavers in the western border regions of China often shared a common nomadic craftsmanship with those in the Caucasus and Turkmenistan. The classic Chinese carpet is quite distinct from those tribal textiles. In most of the Islamic weaving countries, carpets were first and foremost functional items, which formed the main furnishings in the majority of homes. The Chinese, however, began using furniture in the conventional Western sense early on in their history and, for them, carpets were always a purely decorative luxury. In China, carpets were produced in well-organized manufacturing centres under patronage from the emperor and his nobles, and only the wealthiest individuals could afford to own them. The designs, too, were different, shaped by the religions of Buddhism and Taoism, not Islam.

The carpets of India were even less functional than those of China. The weaving tradition is thought to have been brought to India by Mogul invaders in the early sixteenth century and from that time most carpets were woven exclusively for the court. The Moguls came from the Mongol lands to the north of India and had picked up a love of fine weaving, among other things, from the Persians. Once settled in India, the Moguls encouraged imitation of this craft which the native people gradually adapted, producing some very fine pieces in their own right.

This brief survey suggests that the history of carpets has been peculiarly Eastern and generally Islamic. In essence, this impression is correct, but it fails to take one important factor into account. From as early as the eleventh century, when the Crusaders returned home from their military expeditions in the Middle East with carpets among the booty of war, Europeans have been fascinated by oriental carpets. The Venetian merchant and adventurer Marco Polo, when he travelled through Turkey in 1271, wrote that "the best and handsomest carpets in the world are wrought here". And when the British diplomat Sir Anthony Shirley visited Persia in 1599, he was equally complimentary about Persian weaving and returned home laden with gold, jewels and magnificent carpets. Sadly, most of these treasures were stolen in transit.

But the most convincing evidence of European interest can be found in the paintings of those Western nations. From the work of Giotto in the thirteenth century onward, carpets, usually Turkish in origin, appear regularly in paintings. They feature spread before the Virgin and Child or at the feet of kings and queens, draped from the balconies of Italian noblemen or covering tables round which British dignitaries are gathered. Indeed, Hans Holbein the Younger (1497–1543) was so fond of featuring a particular type of predominately red Turkish carpet in his paintings that in time these became known as "Holbeins".

In all these paintings the carpet's role as a status symbol was clear. Oriental rugs were still unusual in Europe and tremendously expensive. They would rarely, if ever, have been walked on but would instead have been displayed with all the reverence their price tags warranted. Their aura of exclusivity ensured that oriental rugs were soon the height of fashion in the West and eagerly sought after by the privileged few who could afford them.

In France these intricately worked carpets became so popular that the flood of money out of the country began to affect the economy. Matters became so serious that in 1608 King Henry IV, anxious to stem the tide, took the unprecedented step of setting up an "oriental carpet" workshop within his own palace walls at the Louvre. He hoped to satisfy his subjects' demand for oriental-style carpets, while keeping the money used to purchase them within French boundaries. These carpets followed genuine oriental weaving techniques but incorporated floral designs by court artists in the French style.

Henry was delighted with the carpets produced and instantly declared that they should be reserved for the exclusive use of the

· · · ·

royal family—thus neatly defeating his own original objective. However, his successor Louis XIII was also interested in the "French orientals" and ordered that production be expanded into an outside workshop. The building chosen for this workshop had once been a soap factory and was still known as La Savonnerie by the locals. The carpets produced there came to be known as "Savonneries" and were Europe's first original carpet designs.

The Savonneries enjoyed a fair measure of success, but still the carpets most coveted by Europeans were from Turkey. The trade paths between Turkey and Europe, via Venice, had been well trodden for centuries so it is not surprising that the majority of carpets which reached the West, at least until the seventeenth century, were of Turkish origin. Consequently, all hand-knotted carpets, even those which had actually been made in Persia or Egypt, were known as "Turkey carpets" and the words "oriental" and "Turkish" were considered synonymous.

Demand for these "orientals" soon exceeded supply. As early as the seventeenth century, Europeans travelled to Turkey to establish local weavers in cottage industries. For the first time, ordinary weavers working at home began to produce carpets with materials provided by contractors who specified their own designs. The European influence on this once exclusively oriental art had begun.

Turkish carpets may have paved the way to Europe for the carpet trade, but Persia was not slow to follow. And, as had happened in the Turkish market, once foreign buyers became more interested in Persian carpets the international traders began influencing carpet design in a bid to make their wares more marketable in the West. In Poland, for example, Persian carpets rapidly became more popular and wealthy families began commissioning carpets, largely from the weaving area of Isfahan. Intended to compliment grand decor in the European style, these fine and richly worked pieces were often woven in silk and adorned with gold and silver threads. The traditionally intricate designs and bright, vibrant colours of Persia were simplified and softened into sweeping floral designs in muted pastel shades. Sometimes family coats-of-arms or national symbols were included in the designs of these carpets, which were found not only in Poland but also in all the great salons of Europe.

This great boom in the carpet market was essentially led by fashion. While it lasted for more than a hundred years, this trend, like so many others, eventually passed. By the eighteenth century, with the increased popularity of neo-classical design, there was little European interest in oriental carpets. The slump in the export market coincided with a decline in the wealth and influence of the Eastern courts and an increase in political unrest in the weaving nations. Without the financial support of their old patrons, the carpet workshops began to decline and with them the production of highly elaborate, court-style carpets.

Large-scale production was no longer an economic proposition, but carpet weaving did not halt altogether. Oriental carpets were still very much a part of daily life in Eastern countries and cottage weaving industries continued to thrive. As the European influence on design lessened, weavers returned to the robust colours and patterns of their heritage.

It was not until the nineteenth century that oriental carpets began to arouse European interest once again, and after a hundred years of abstinence wealthy Westerners rapidly regained their taste for them. This return to fashion was probably begun by the intrepid, and often eccentric, Victorian travellers who at this time began to explore the Middle and Far East. The carpets they brought back were not the delicate and refined court carpets, but those richly coloured and boldly patterned village and tribal pieces that had been shunned as crude by earlier Europeans. The Victorians, however, loved them. These vibrant pieces complimented the heavy dark furniture and rich velvets of Victorian taste and demand grew rapidly.

The resurgence in popularity of oriental carpets opened up rich new business possibilities for those with an entrepreneurial streak. There was no real organized carpet industry in the Middle East at this time and demand was far exceeding supply. In response to this hole in the market, dealers operating in the Tabriz area of Persia came up with the idea of organizing production into large-scale workshops or factories as they are sometimes called. By gathering a large number of looms under one roof and paying the weavers a weekly rate, the factory owners could react rapidly and accurately to the demands of the market. So successful were these first ventures that the concept rapidly spread throughout Persia and into other weaving nations. The demand for carpets was seemingly insatiable and importers also sent their local representatives ever farther afield in search of tribal rugs. They bought every kind of knotted item they could lay their hands on, including the great saddle bags and tent ornaments of the nomads. These items were usually cut up to make small mats and ornaments.

In the rush to buy, there was almost no attempt to catalogue and record the provenance of these pieces. Local traders knew little about them and Western buyers knew even less. Some records were kept on the commercially produced items, but the only information available today about the village and tribal pieces snapped up at that time has been handed down by word of mouth through the great family trading dynasties which were then beginning to be established. These categories were based on neither history nor science. Instead they were shaped by limited information about where the carpets had been exported from and any design similarities they might have with other pieces. They were also influenced by individual perceptions of size, colour, design—and the occasional bit of presumption.

At times this lack of knowledge led to some mistakes. At the *Exposition Universelle* in Paris in 1866, a Polish nobleman and oriental rug enthusiast put his fine collection of seventeenth-century Isfahan carpets on display. Journalists reviewing the exhibition saw Poland listed as the country of origin for this exhibit and wrote about the beautiful collection of Polish, or "Polonaise", carpets. By the time their mistake was spotted, the incorrect categorization had already become accepted. Even now, that kind of seventeenth-century Isfahan carpet is known in the trade as a "Polonaise".

Despite its relative ignorance, the Western market was still increasingly enthusiastic. By the second half of the nineteenth century, even conservative, middle-class homes contained at least one oriental rug. Eventually, however, the rush to supply this continuing demand did begin to affect quality. Weaving is a labour-intensive craft and, once production had been intensified in factory workshops, the only other way to increase output was to cut corners. Knotting became coarser and designs were inaccurately reproduced, but the most devastating development of all was the discovery of artificial dyes. Until this time yarn had been slowly and painstakingly tinted with natural dyes, but in the 1860s the first synthetic colours were discovered and soon found their way into oriental carpets

After the initial excitement over the discovery, disillusion rapidly set in. The so-called "aniline" colours were harsh, unstable and, on occasion, actually damaging to the wool. This episode gave the oriental carpet industry a nasty jolt. Aniline dyes were banned and general weaving standards began to rise once again.

New and vastly improved dyes were discovered that could rival natural dyestuffs for quality and far exceed them in spectrum. Traditional designs were respected again and reproduced with skill. Carpet output settled at a high enough level to satisfy Western demand—but without compromising the quality that generated that demand in the first place. In recent years, an increasingly discerning Western market has grown to value oriental carpets for what they are, not what Western influence might shape them into being.

However, what should be a uniquely harmonious time in the history of the carpet looks set to become the hour of its greatest trial. The threat is now economic, not artistic. As the Western lifestyle becomes a global goal, the labour-intensive craft of carpet making is in very real danger of dying out. Families are leaving the country in search of prosperity in the cities and there is no longer time in their lives for weaving. Women, whose families have woven beautiful carpets for generations, are abandoning their looms for the factory conveyor belt. The craft of carpet making is so deeply embedded in its society that it has managed to survive centuries of unrest, a harsh landscape and the vagaries of fashion. Ironically, it may yet be destroyed by the very contact with the West which has made it so valuable to preserve.

$\mathcal{H}$OW CARPETS ARE MADE

nderstanding is one of the first steps toward true appreciation. Thus, the carpet enthusiast needs to learn a little about the materials and mechanics of carpet making before he or she can make an informed purchase or a satisfactory artistic judgement.

Very little equipment is required to make a carpet and the weaving skills are remarkably basic, but, as anyone who has tried their hand at this art can testify, a knotted carpet is much more than the sum of its parts. There is an intangible extra element, a feeling for this craft bred over generations, which lifts the simple knotting of wool tufts on to a network of base threads from the mechanically mundane to the artistically sublime.

The weaver's loom

Every carpet starts with a loom, a simple frame which gives the base threads the necessary tension to allow knots to be tied on them. The most basic form is the horizontal loom used by nomadic tribal weavers. This is nothing more than two stout poles, often poplar trunks which usually grow straight and are common in rug weaving areas. The poles form the top and bottom of the loom and are pegged out on the ground at a distance slightly greater than the intended length of the finished carpet. Long threads, usually of wool, are wrapped tightly between the poles and spaced side by side, evenly and closely, to the desired width of the finished carpet. These vertical threads are the warps and once these are in place the weaver is ready to begin.

The weaver works kneeling on the ground. The next task is to create a firm foundation at the bottom end of the loom. This is done by weaving a ball of thread over the first warp, under the second, over the third and so on. These horizontal threads are called wefts.

Once the weaver reaches the other side, she works the weft back again, reversing the order of the weave. This time she takes the weft under those warps that she worked over the first time, and over the ones she went under, slowly building up a basic woven material. This flat weave foundation, called a *kilim*, is continued for anything from 2·5 to 15 centimetres (1 to 6 inches) or more, according to local style and the whim of the weaver.

Now the weaver is ready to tie her first row of knots. There are basically two kinds of knot, the Persian, or asymmetrical, knot, and the Turkish, or symmetrical, knot. In fact, these names have no geographic connection, so the knot the weaver uses is decided by the custom within his or her tribe, not by the tribe's location. Some weavers have a special hooked tool to help tie the knots, but most simply use their fingers to wrap each length of woollen pile thread round two adjacent warps. As each knot is completed, the trailing ends are cut with a knife, leaving a shaggy pile about 7·5 to 10 centimetres (3 to 4 inches) long. The weaver works methodically across the entire width of the carpet, tying a single row of knots.

Once a row of knots has been completed, the weaver works one or sometimes two or three more weft threads across the width of the loom. Then, using a comblike tool which slots between the warp threads, she beats down hard on the wefts to lock the knots below them into place.

Work then continues, alternating single rows of knots with one or more lines of weft threads, until the work measures 7·5 to 10 centimetres (3 to 4 inches). The weaver then takes a special pair of heavy scissors, with a guard on their upper blade, and carefully cuts back the pile to a length of about 2·5 centimetres (1 inch). The details of the pattern are revealed for the first time from an area that was previously a jumble of trailing threads.

A skilled weaver can tie some 20 knots a minute, but it may still be several months before the rug is complete. Once the finished length has been reached, the weaver works another length of flat weave, or *kilim*, to secure the top of the carpet in the same way as the bottom and the work is complete.

The finished carpet is cut from the horizontal beams which have kept it stretched tight and straight, and the trailing ends of

A typical oriental carpet.

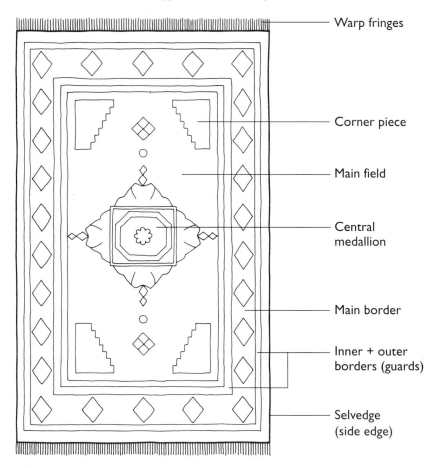

Warp fringes

Corner piece

Main field

Central medallion

Main border

Inner + outer borders (guards)

Selvedge (side edge)

the warp threads are neatened. These now form the fringes that are an intrinsic part of every oriental carpet. They may be plaited, knotted or left plain, according to the traditions of the area, but the top fringe is nearly always longer than the bottom fringe.

The carpet is then dunked in a stream to cleanse it of the grime which has accumulated over the months of making, and laid out in the sun to dry. The pile is given a final trim with shaving sweeps from a huge, flat-bladed knife and the finished piece is finally revealed in all its glory.

Production of the more sophisticated village and city rugs varies only in the type of loom used, the quality of the yarns and the degree of technical skill of the weaver. The looms of nomadic people are designed to be easily transported. If the tribe has to move on before a carpet is finished, the pegs holding the top and bottom beams of the loom in place are lifted. The beams, complete with the warp threads and partially completed carpet, are rolled up into a neat bundle which is relatively light and easy to carry.

A village weaver at her loom.

Village looms, in contrast, are designed to be permanent structures and are made either in the main room of the house or in the yard outside. In such enclosed areas, where space is at a premium, it is logical that such looms should be upright. The simple vertical loom of the village follows the same principles as the horizontal nomadic loom, but, instead of pegs holding the top and bottom beams in place on the ground, two strong vertical beams are fixed in place and the horizontal beams are lashed to them, forming a rough rectangular frame. The village weaver sits down to work at a bench before her loom. As the carpet progresses, the bench is gradually raised ever higher to keep the weaver on a level with her work. By the time the carpet is finished she may be perched some 3 metres (10 feet) up—the length of the carpet.

While this arrangement causes few problems for village weavers, who generally produce small to medium-sized pieces, it could become dangerous for city weavers at work on really large carpets. Consequently, a number of refinements have been developed which allow the partially completed carpet to be scrolled down while the weavers continue to work with their feet safely on the ground. Sometimes the warps completely encircle the top and bottom beams in unbroken loops, so that the beams can simply be rolled in tandem to lower the working level on the front of the loom, while the completed portion passes under the lower beam and gradually rises up behind. Using this system, it is possible to weave a carpet that is twice the length of the height of the loom.

Alternatively, a roller beam loom may be used. On this, extra-long warp threads are fixed in the normal way to the bottom beam, while the slack is wound out of the way round the top beam until the warps are at a working tension. As work progresses, a length of completed rug is wound out of the way round the bottom beam at the same time as fresh portions of the warp threads are unwound from the top beam.

The disadvantage of both continuous and roller beam looms is that the weaver cannot see the entire carpet as she works, since most of the completed area is wound out of the way. A nomadic weaver could not cope without seeing all the work stretched out before her. Tribal weavers make up their designs as they go along and, although they use traditional motifs and combinations, the design is ultimately decided by an instinctive sense of what looks right on a particular rug.

Village weavers follow their own instincts and taste in colour, but the designs they use have generally been inherited from previous generations. They learn the designs by watching their own parents at work, but may also follow written instructions similar to a knitting pattern—work one red, five blue, eight red and so on. Village weavers do not always have a picture of what the finished design should look like and there are carpets in which the design mysteriously distorts before returning to a recognizable pattern. This shows that the weaver had a momentary lapse of concentration and missed or repeated a line of the pattern by mistake.

City weavers are paid by the day for their skills and work in large, organized workshops. They follow a type of graphic instruction known as a cartoon. This is a precise picture of the finished design laid out on graph paper on which every square of the grid represents single knot of the finished carpet. These cartoons are created by highly skilled, and highly paid, designers. Only with such a plan is it possible to achieve the symmetry and precision of a perfectly executed city rug.

Types of knots

As already mentioned, there are only two types of knot used in the creation of oriental carpets. These two knots are called by many different names, however. The Turkish knot is also described as a Ghiordes or symmetrical knot. The Persian knot is termed a Senneh or asymmetrical knot. While the geographical names have no significance, the descriptive names—symmetrical or closed and symmetrical or open—are quite accurate. The descriptive names are less often used within the trade, however, so it pays to be familiar with all the terms.

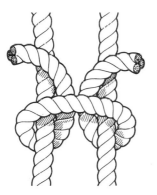

Turkish, or Ghiordes, knot   Persian, or Senneh, knot

The type of knot a carpet is made with is an important identifying feature when establishing its provenance. Although Persian weavers do not always use the Persian knot, nor Turkish weavers the Turkish knot, individual weaving areas do always work with the same kind of knot. This can be confusing. For example, carpets from Senneh are generally made with the Ghiordes, or Turkish, knot rather than with the Senneh, or Persian, knot.

It is possible to tell which type of knot has been used by examining a carpet carefully, but this is a talent which generally comes only years of practice. Do not be deterred—everyone has to start somewhere. Push back the pile to reveal the base of the knot and try to determine how these threads wind round the warps.

At this stage, bear in mind that there is an additional refinement which may be applied to the tying of a Persian knot that significantly alters its shape. This refinement is not applied to a Turkish knot. When a standard Persian knot is completed, the two warp threads it encloses lie side by side. But, if the weaver pulls harder on one end of the pile thread than on the other, this will cause one warp thread to rise above the other. In extreme cases, the two warps end up one on top of the other.

Flat weaves

Some flat weaves, or *kilims*, are quicker and less costly to produce than pile carpets. They are generally woven by nomads, who use these soft and flexible textiles to make bags, trappings and animal harnesses. Their designs are bold and primitive and inspire passion in enthusiasts, but, technically speaking, *kilims* are simpler, more straightforward weaves than knotted carpets. *Kilims* are also made in villages and very occasionally in cities such as Bijar and Senneh.

In its simplest form a *kilim* is identical front and back, since the designs are created by winding coloured weft threads in and out of the warps. Each differently coloured weft is taken only as far across the width of the *kilim* as the design demands and then brought back on itself to create a solid block of colour. This technique results in vertical slits being created wherever two rectangular blocks of colour meet. These slits make the *kilim* particularly flexible, which is a useful quality for nomads on the move. But slits are not desirable in all instances—for example, if the *kilim* is to be made into a bag—and there a couple of ways the weaver can avoid them.

The first, and simplest, way is to weave only horizontal bands of colour that extend the entire width of the *kilim*. Alternatively, the impact of the slits can be lessened by ensuring that blocks of colour are always worked on diagonal lines.

More complex designs require a slightly different technique. Instead of the two coloured wefts simply reversing back on themselves at adjacent warps, the wefts may either be wrapped round a common warp, or round each other, at the point where they meet. This creates slight ridges in the surface and the most technically advanced *kilim* weavers use or even exaggerate these ridges to enhance their designs.

Materials

Carpets may be made solely from wool or from combinations of wool, cotton and silk. Some rough tribal carpets may even incorporate goat or camel hair for greater strength—and for greater economy as the wool may come from the weavers' own animals. Throughout the weaving nations it is common to find wool pile knotted on to cotton warp and weft threads, and areas of silk pile may be added to highlight the design. Silk can be used for the warp threads and produces a strong foundation. Very fine knots can be made with silk. Carpets are also made with a pure silk pile on cotton or silk warp and wefts. Persian silk pile carpets are almost always made on a silk base, but carpets from other countries sometimes use silk on a cotton base.

Cotton is increasingly common in the warp and weft threads of oriental carpets, not only in those from India and Pakistan where it is widely available, but also in Turkish and Persian workshop carpets. Rural weavers have been slower to switch to cotton, preferring their homegrown wool to bought-in cotton, but slowly they, too, are being swept along by the trend. There are good reasons for the change. While a wool foundation may buckle and warp, a cotton base is firm yet flexible and is widely believed to grip the knots of a woollen pile more strongly. Almost all city rugs are made on cotton or silk.

Less desirable is the use of mercerized cotton—cotton which has been treated to give it a silky sheen—for the pile in cheap workshop carpets. These carpets are intended to look like silk for a fraction of the price, However, the effect does not last long once the carpet is walked on and if you want a carpet to enjoy for years to come, avoid these mercerized cotton or "art silk" pieces.

Even real silk pieces can vary in quality. Silk is, of course, the thread extruded by silk worms to bind themselves into their cocoons. When this fine thread is unravelled for weaving, the first lengths are fine and even and these are used to make the best quality silk material. The nearer the thread gets to the base of the cocoon the more erratic its quality becomes. This rather knubbly thread is called slub silk and, although with careful pressing it can retain a certain sheen, a slub silk pile carpet quickly loses its lustre when it is ruffled and walked on. It is not enough for a carpet to have a silk pile; it must be good quality silk.

Quality is also important in wool pile. Good wool feels soft, springy and slightly oily to the touch. Inferior wool pile feels brittle and dry. Apart from the obvious tactile attractions of a high quality pile, it has the resilience to improve over the years as passing feet buff it to a deep and lasting lustre, highly prized by connoisseurs.

The manner of spinning also affects the appearance and durability of the finished piece. Handspun yarn, even today often produced using a primitive spindle, always has slight variations in width which give a certain dynamism to the finished pile. Machine-spun yarn is absolutely consistent and, while this quality control assures that it is certainly better than poorly handspun yarn, purists would argue that it can never compete with a skilfully handspun thread.

❦

COLOUR AND DESIGN

🌿

An appreciation of the weaving technique involved in making a carpet is important, and the style and degree of skill displayed are valuable clues as to the provenance of a piece and its market value. But it is also interesting to know something about the sizes, colours and designs of carpets.

Size of carpets

Oriental rugs come in an enormous range of sizes and shapes. In fact, the only physical limit to the size of an oriental carpet is the size of the loom on which it is woven. Within this limitation, a wide variety of shapes can be created. Working on a loom prepared in the normal fashion, the weaver simply expands and contracts the area of weaving to make the chosen shape. Circular rugs are not uncommon and animal trappings, often strangely shaped, can frequently be seen, both in the East, where they serve an obvious function, and in the West, where their bright colours and intriguing forms have made them popular ornaments for years. However, most carpets are rectangular and come in a standard range of sizes. In Europe and Iran anything up to 244 x 152 centimetres (96 x 60 inches) is referred to as a rug. Larger pieces are called carpets. In the United States, all handwoven carpets are referred to as rugs.

The smallest common size is the *pushti*, a measure of 90 x 60 centimetres (36 x 24 inches). *Pushti* also means "back" in Farsi, and *pushti* rugs are traditionally used to cover the cushions against which seated guests lean when visiting a Persian house. Moving up in size is the *zaronim*, at 152 x 90 centimetres (60 x 36 inches) and the *dozar*, at 213 x 122 centimetres (84 x 48 inches). A *zar* is a traditional measure, equal to one metre. *Zaronim* means one and a half *zars* and *dozar* means two *zars* (see glossary).

....

Traditionally, most village rugs were *kelehs*, or *keleggi*, about 274 x 152 centimetres (108 x 60 inches) long. Persian rooms tend to be long and thin and the time-honoured arrangement was to lay one of these large carpets across one end, with two long thin rugs butting against it at right angles and spreading the length of the room.

As the West became more interested in oriental carpets so traditional proportions were modified to suit the squarer plan of European-style rooms. Since the middle of the nineteenth century the most commonly woven sizes have been 366 x 274 centimetres (144 x 108 inches) and 300 x 200 centimetres (118 x 79 inches). Western interest also led to an increasing number of special size commissions from wealthy enthusiasts and it is now possible to buy carpets of almost any dimensions, although each weaving region still has a certain range of characteristic sizes. On occasion, new uses have been found for the old shapes. For example, *kenarehs*, or runners as they are often called, are now popular in the West for halls, corridors and even staircases.

Colour

Colour is an essential ingredient of the oriental carpet. Whether in the limited but bold palette of the tribal carpet or in the amazing complexity of a city piece, in which 20 or more different colours can sit harmoniously side by side, skilful use of colour is the mark of a truly great oriental carpet.

Historically, all dyes were collected from naturally occurring substances. For instance, red might come the ground roots of madder plants, blue from the indigo plant, yellow from saffron, and brown from walnut shells. The application of these dyes was a skilled business and within communities of any size there was always one family that specialized in the art of dyeing. Even the normally self-sufficient nomads would come to these professionals for shades that were difficult to achieve. In the hands of a master dyer, yarns could be transformed into a rainbow of jewel-bright hues. Although these colours faded slightly over the years, this was seen not as a technical failing but as a desirable mellowing, producing an exquisitely harmonious balance of tone and colour.

In 1856, the first synthetic dye was discovered by a scientist who was actually trying to synthesize quinine. That first synthetic colour was a vivid shade of mauve, but from this starting point the spectrum was rapidly expanded. These aniline dyes were strong and bright, and became very popular. The extent of their use, however, was limited for many years by their high cost and the new colours were often used to highlight details rather than for whole carpets.

Yet even while the use of aniline dyes was becoming more and more common, and the cost of the dyes was dropping, defects began to emerge. Many of the colours proved to be extremely light sensitive and did not merely fade but lost colour completely, leaving an unappealing range of muddy shades. Few of the dyes were colour-fast and colours would bleed if a carpet became wet. Perhaps worse still, it soon became clear that aniline-dyed yarn disintegrated with alarming speed.

Aniline dyes were dropped from use as rapidly as they had caught on. In Persia the dyes were banned by the government, anxious to preserve the country's reputation as a producer of fine carpets. In other countries, the weavers were left to make their own decisions. Most soon realized the commercial sense of a voluntary ban, although a few weavers continued to take the short-term view.

It takes a long time for a carpet to get from the weaver's loom to a Western shop, and by the time the Western buyers had learned about the problems of aniline dyes, new and improved synthetic dyes had begun to emerge. But the prejudice against synthetics was by then so entrenched that Western dealers tended to encourage their customers in the belief that the carpets they were buying had been dyed with natural substances, rather than risk an explanation of the genuine merits of the new dyes.

The fact that this minor deception could succeed at all is in itself a testimony to the high quality of the new colours known as chrome dyes. These had been developed in the late nineteenth century, but it was only after the Second World War that their use became widespread. Nowadays, most carpets are woven from a combination of natural- and chrome-dyed wool. Unlike their aniline predecessors, these chrome dyes are light and colour fast and have little or no effect on wool quality.

Some purists say that the chrome dyes are a little too colour fast, preventing modern rugs from mellowing in the way that the old naturally dyed pieces did. However, chrome dyes offer an enormous range of colours and, if skilfully applied, can rival even the best natural dyes for beauty.

Generally speaking, there is little point worrying about how a carpet was dyed. There are countless examples of inferior dyeing with natural materials and equal numbers of exquisite effects from chrome dyes. Look at the quality of the colour and ignore its origin.

Abrash

As you examine the colour in oriental pieces more closely, you may notice that large areas of a single colour are slightly mottled or even striped in a number of subtly different tones. This effect is called an abrash and is highly prized by many connoisseurs for the wonderful vitality it brings to nominally monotone areas.

Abrash is caused either by an uneven take-up of dye on handspun yarn, or by uneven fading in the finished piece. It is most pronounced on handspun, vegetable-dyed yarn. Conversely, with machine-spun, chemically dyed pieces, abrash is rare, although if synthetic dyes are applied by hand to handspun yarn the finished result is as full of charming inconsistencies as an all-natural piece.

Occasionally, an abrash may be deliberate and obvious, perhaps in an effort to cash in on the popularity of natural abrash. In general, rugs with deliberate abrash are best avoided.

Chemical washing

Chemical washing is the name given to the bleaching process devised earlier this century to tone down the bright colours of new oriental carpets in order to make them more appealing to Western buyers. In its mildest form this process imitates, and of course speeds up, the natural mellowing which so enhances a carpet's appearance over the years. At the extreme, it can completely change the colours in a carpet, turning bright primaries into soft pastels and removing some colours completely to leave areas of off-white. No chemical washing process can be said to be good for a carpet and heavy washing can virtually destroy the resilience of the pile, drastically reducing the life expectancy of a piece.

Design—geometric and curvilinear

Though the huge number of different oriental carpet designs can be bewildering for the beginner, it is possible to make sense of it all by being aware of one simple fact: almost every oriental carpet can be described as basically geometric or curvilinear—or at least leaning to one category or the other.

Geometric carpets are generally tribal or village in origin. Their angular designs are a product of both their coarse weave, which renders curves impossible, and the weavers' habit of producing their designs from memory as the carpet progresses, which makes fine draughtsmanship equally unattainable. In place of planning there is spontaneity and a wilful and exuberant spirit that sings out from these simple forms.

Curvilinear carpets are produced almost exclusively in the city workshops. A very fine knot count is necessary to create such delicate curves and arabesques and the intricate designs are the product of careful planning, usually by a master designer. The results are controlled with a courtly elegance and, at their best, can be absolutely sublime.

Individual design elements may be used in both categories, but clearly their shape and impact will be modified. At their best, curvilinear carpets are like fine Old Master paintings, impeccably crafted and exquisitely worked. Fine tribal rugs, on the other hand, have much in common with the work of modernist, twentieth-century artists. (Indeed, tribal carpets, along with other forms of tribal art, have had an acknowledged influence on these artists.) Their primitive designs combine raw power with charming naivety.

While true carpet connoisseurs appreciate the beauty of both design categories, they will almost always feel a natural bias toward one or the other. This instinctive inclination is felt just as strongly by absolute beginners and so provides the first clear signpost in the complex and confusing world of carpets.

The rich patterns of oriental carpets are more than mere decorative devices. Just as every picture tells a story, carpet designs have been shaped by a cultural symbolism which has developed over the centuries. Though the "meaning" of many of these designs is rarely understood by the weavers who reproduce them today, this does not reduce their interest to the person looking at the carpets, nor their importance as symbols of an ancient tradition.

An exhaustive survey of patterns and possible meanings would fill this book many times over, but it is possible to identify a handful of the most frequently occurring motifs and designs.

Motifs

Of the motifs, the *herati* is the most common pattern element. Although it has many variations, the basic structure—a diamond, enclosing a rosette, and embellished with two smaller rosettes at each of its four corners and a serrated "leaf" lying along each side—is always recognizable. Some scholars argue that these "leaves" are actually fish and call this motif the *mahi*, or fish, design. Their theory ties in with an ancient legend that whenever there is a full moon, all the fish of the

Herati motif

lakes rise to the surface to admire their reflections in the water. Viewed in this way, the abstract *herati* motif becomes a wonderfully vivid picture.

Single *herati* motifs can be incorporated into many designs, but there is also a design in which repeated *herati* motifs are placed in formation to make a linking pattern with no loose ends. This design reflects the Islamic view of the interdependence of all sections of the universe. The *herati* is also combined and modified with a vase motif to form an all-over pattern called the *mina khani*, or daisy, design.

The *gol* motif   The *boteh* motif

This design is used by weavers throughout the East but is particularly popular in the Persian weaving town of Veramin.

The *gol*, a word which means "flower" in Persian, is another common motif. Basically a stylized flower, the *gol* is generally agreed to represent a rose. In Persia this is a potent symbol of life since the rose, like life, is beautiful but bears many thorns and once picked soon fades and dies.

The *boteh* motif is most familiar to Westerners as the basic element of the paisley pattern. In the world of carpets, the *boteh* has been variously interpreted as a droplet of water, stylized almond, pine cone or palmetto leaf. *Boteh* actually means "leaf" in Persian, which adds credibility to the palmetto leaf interpretation.

The basic *boteh* may be used in an all-over design of horizontal rows, with the *botehs* in alternate lines facing in opposite directions. *Botehs* may also be arranged in a set pattern to form a further motif, which is called a *hashtguli* or "eight

The palmette motif

flower" motif. It is interesting to note that the *boteh* is common on Persian carpets but rarely appears in any form on Turkish carpets.

The palmette, another classic motif, is thought to represent the opium poppy, long cultivated in Persia. It is associated with meditation, mysticism and trances.

Tribal motifs are more primitive in some ways. A stylized dog was traditionally woven to keep thieves, illness and evil spirits away. A woven tarantula frightened off the real thing. Roosters, held by many tribes to be the embodiment of evil, served in the same way to keep the effects of evil away from the household. Blue beads, yet another powerful force against evil, were often sewn into the borders of a rug. Pomegranates represented fruitfulness and fertility, while pictures of houses were reminders of a permanent way of life far removed from the nomadic habits of most tribes.

Designs

The *mihrab*, or prayer arch, is an integral part of every prayer rug. Whether stylized or refined, its form is instantly recognizable and echoes the architecture of the mosque. Sometimes a lantern hangs from the apex of the arch. Once again, this is basically a pictorial representation of the lamps which hang from typically long fine chains in mosques.

Prayer rugs were once common but are seldom seen today, even in Muslim countries. The elements of their design are rich with religious meaning. A pair of hands is often worked on either side of the arch, a design known as "The Hand of Fatima". This could simply be a guide for the worshipper to position himself when he kneels to pray. However, the five fingers of the hand traditionally represent the five members of the family of the prophet Mohammed—

The *mihrab*

Mohammed himself, his cousin and son-in-law Ali, his daughter Fatima and her sons Hasan and Hossein—and the five basic principles of Islam—faith, prayer, pilgrimage, fasting and charity. The same philosophies lie behind the motif of the five-toothed comb, which may also appear on prayer rugs. The significance of the comb is reinforced by the Muslim belief that cleanliness is next to godliness.

The tree of life is another popular religious design and may sometimes be positioned under a *mihrab*. The tree of life is common to many cultures but has special meaning for Muslims. For them, living generally in arid lands, the tree of life is a symbol of a green,

The tree of life   The vase of immortality

leafy paradise, promised in the Koran to those who truly believe.

The vase of immortality has similar symbolic significance and it, too, is frequently coupled with a *mihrab*. The vase is usually shaped like a Greek urn and filled to overflowing with beautiful flowers. In a variation on this design, the flower-filled vase is reduced in size and used to form a repeat pattern that covers the ground of the carpet. Some scholars believe that the vase pattern originated in Chinese weaving, where it was strictly representational, not symbolic. Persian weavers, they argue, borrowed the design and gradually imbued it with their own symbolic significance. There are also a number of popular variations on the repeat pattern vase design, the most common of which is called the *zeli-soltan* design—*zeli-soltan* means in the shadow of the sultan or king.

The medallion design, is, perhaps the one that immediately springs to mind when we picture an oriental carpet. Although as a design it appears completely abstract, the central point of the medallion is said to represent either the all-seeing eye of God, or a lotus blossom—long considered a sacred symbol since it grows in the mud but turns its face up to the heavens. It could also be architecturally inspired, recalling the elaborate designs of mosque ceilings. Whatever its origins, the medallion frequently appears in a design with quarter medallions in the four corners. This overall pattern is often used to embellish the covers of holy books, in particular the Koran.

In contrast, the hunting design appears to the casual observer to be far removed from the religious concerns of so many other motifs. In fact, the hunt, traditionally the sport of kings, is one of the pastimes promised to the faithful in Paradise, according to the Koran. Although these woven hunting scenes seem unnaturally stuffed with prey, they are probably quite accurate historically. Real hunts were highly organized affairs, in preparation for which countless small animals were driven into a narrow valley that was then sealed off, guaranteeing every participant a good catch.

Compared with the bustle of the naturalistic hunt scenes, garden design carpets can seem static and stylized. In fact, garden carpets are remarkably accurate pictures of the Persian style of garden. The borders of the carpet are the boundaries of the garden, criss-crossing irrigation channels divide the field into a grid and in the squares between lie plants, trees, animals and, occasionally, even a house. Garden carpets are also popular with some of the tribes, in particular the Bakhtiari who, with their nomadic lifestyle, could only dream of owning a real garden.

Some designs have even been borrowed from other countries, such as the *gol farangi* which is based on the elegant French floral Savonnerie design. *Gol farangi* roughly translates as "foreign flower/rose" and the design, with its stylized cabbage roses is one interesting example of the orientalization of a Western motif.

Chinese designs

Despite the difference between tribal and town symbolism, the designs of Muslim countries are fundamentally united by the shared religion. Chinese symbolism is usually rather different, however, since it is shaped by the predominately Confucian, Buddhist and Taoist traditions.

Perhaps the best known Chinese motif of all is the yin-yang symbol, which represents the interaction, even the interdependence, of light and dark, heaven and earth, male and female. The dragon and the phoenix symbolize a similar interaction but also represent the emperor and empress. Cloud patterns symbolize heaven and are frequently woven into borders, forming a protective ring round the characters and symbols on the field. In fact, almost every element of a Chinese carpet design carries some symbolic significance. Experts can read whole messages within designs that appear purely decorative to the untrained eye.

Borders

Almost all oriental carpet designs are finished off by a series of borders, or patterned bands. These are a foil for the main carpet design, much like a picture frame, but are often highly decorative in their own right.

The number of borders can range from none to eight or more. Usually there is one main stripe, with a number of lesser stripes on either side of it. Precisely how many borders are worked is often a clue to the provenance of a carpet, as is the style of decoration within those borders. The range of motifs used in border design tends to be somewhat limited. The most common features are flower motifs, Chinese cloud bands, elongated cartouches and the so-called running dog design, which is a simple repeat motif of hook-topped lines.

ℬUYING A CARPET

🍃

B uying a carpet can, and should, be fun. But it can also be a bewildering business. The range of size, colour, design, quality and price is enormous, so the first step is to learn how to narrow your search area. Once within your chosen boundaries, explore at your leisure until you find just what you want.

Narrowing the choice

There are certain things which you must consider when buying a carpet. First, decide what size you are looking for. If you want a carpet for a certain room or area, measure that area thoroughly, taking into account any awkward corners and fireplaces, so that you know the maximum and minimum sizes possible (*see* pp. 25–26 for information on carpet sizes.)

Second, decide on the colour range you would prefer if you are buying a carpet to fit an existing colour scheme—whether you want something with strong, vivid hues or softer, more muted shades. A better plan, if possible, is to buy the carpet first and match everything else to it. Carpets are heirlooms; they last for generations and are not as often changed as curtains or chair covers. Let yourself fall in love with the carpet that most attracts you and fit other furnishings around it.

Third, know your budget. Tell the salesman the maximum you want to spend so he can show you pieces within your price range.

Once you have thought about size, colour and budget, the next point to decide is whether you want to buy a city or a village weaving. The majority of city rugs are fine, intricate weaves, with curvilinear, symmetrical patterns. Most are in standard sizes, conforming to the metric system. Village rugs, which include nomadic and tribal weavings, are generally coarser and more primitive, with thicker pile. Designs are usually non-symmetric, often eccentric and nearly always geometric or semi-geometric.

As you begin to look at carpets you will quickly decide which styles you find most attractive. Photographs, such as those in this book, are useful to help you clarify the types of designs and carpets that appeal to you. However, remember that the colours of oriental carpets are so subtle that they vary in different lights and from different angles. Carpets really need to be seen and touched to be fully appreciated.

Where to buy

The next decision you must make is where you are going to shop. Most large towns and cities now have a number of oriental carpet shops, from tiny grottoes emblazoned with bright orange "sale" stickers to elegant emporiums stocking only the very best pieces. Any shop which permanently displays "sale" signs should be given a wide berth. Carpets are enduring commodities which hold, and usually increase, their value over the years. And as labour costs go up so do carpet prices. No price could ever be significantly reduced unless the piece had been damaged or was overpriced in the first place.

Department stores are convenient for some people. They offer a basic range of commercial carpets, but these are sold as mere floor coverings not as beautiful objects of art to be treasured. For really fine oriental carpets, go to a specialist shop and you will be amazed to see just how exquisite the best orientals can be. Of course, some pieces will be very expensive, but at least you can appreciate the scope of the art. The specialist shops also stock a range of moderately priced pieces and in the end they are probably the best choice. There you can be guided by an expert carpet salesman, whose knowledge and experience is extremely valuable to you as a buyer.

Whatever your budget, you would be well advised to avoid auctions. Auction houses range from the highly respectable, internationally known names to fly-by-night tricksters, who set up in hotels and halls and advertise "bankrupt stock" or "port clearance sales". But at any auction the buyer has to cope with the same obstacles—there is limited viewing time in which to examine a carpet and it is easy to get carried away and overbid. Once a purchase has been made at an auction it cannot be returned. This system protects the auction house, but the buyer has no guarantee that the piece is what it says it is. The prices may seem cheap but there is an old saying—"I am not rich enough to afford cheap goods". You would not expect to buy 22-carat gold for the price of 9-carat and with rugs, too, you get what you pay for. A good rug may cost a fair amount, but you will have value for money.

If you are going to visit the Middle East, you may decide to buy a carpet on your travels. However, you may not get the bargains you hoped for by cutting out the middle men. As a tourist and a carpet-buying novice, you are unlikely to negotiate such a good deal with the vendor as an experienced buyer would do and you may have to pay for shipping and import duties on top. That being said, the whole process can be a lot of fun and, if you choose well, the carpet you buy will be the best of souvenirs. Always buy from reputable showrooms so that you can go back to them if you have any problems.

What to look for

When looking at carpets you need to consider certain factors to help you judge their quality. First, look at the quality of the material and of the weave as well as the degree of skill in weaving. Examine the dyes that have been applied and the condition that the rug is in. Find out the age of the piece and the region it comes from, which may determine the overall balance and design. Remember, too, that carpets are made by individual artists and each one is different. Two pieces may have been made in the same village or city but not have the same value.

Beware of copies. Persian carpets are made by skilled artists, but copies are made in other countries, sometimes even by child labour, and these never match the beauty and quality of the originals. Such copies may be a fraction of the price of a real Persian rug but cannot be called good value. After a few years of use they become shabby and the pile loses its strength. Persian rugs, however, look better and better as they are used and the colours become increasingly mellow as they age.

The type of knot used, whether Persian or Turkish, is irrelevant to the value of the carpets. But in certain pieces—such as modern Persian city carpets and silk carpets from Hereke in Turkey—the density of knots is of great importance in determining the quality of the weave. (In older city pieces and village and tribal carpets, however, knot density is *not* a factor in assessing the quality of carpets and does not affect their value.)

Knot density can be measured quite simply. Turn the carpet over and, using a tape measure or ruler, measure a horizontal strip of 2·5 centimetres (1 inch) and count the knots it contains. Then measure 2·5 centimetres (1 inch) vertically and count the knots that contains. Once you have both a horizontal and a vertical count, multiply the two figures to give the number of knots per 2·5-centimetre square (1 square inch).

This measurement may range from tens to hundreds of knots. Tribal carpets tend to have low counts, while on some city carpets the count is very high, but this does not mean that tribal carpets are inferior. Tribal and village carpets are not judged by their knot density and some can be more expensive than fine city rugs.

Look at the age given for the carpet. For example, some weaving areas only started production 40 or 50 years ago, so anything from that area that is said to be older is a fake. If you have managed to narrow your choice down to a specific weaving area, do as much homework as you can to protect yourself from such inaccuracies.

In any event, when you do buy a carpet, be sure to obtain a Certificate of Authentication, which states the approximate age and origin of the piece. You can feel quite confident that the details the certificate bears are accurate to the best of the dealer's knowledge. He certainly would not wish to risk his reputation. If you do have an independent authentication carried out that concludes origins other than those stated in your certificate, you have strong grounds for taking the carpet back to the dealer who sold it to you.

With authenticity assured, the condition of a carpet is of paramount concern. Don't be tempted to think that a worn carpet must be old and therefore valuable. An old carpet may be worn, but not all worn carpets are old. Buy a carpet in a poor state of repair and your investment will simply unravel before your eyes.

Sound warp and weft threads are essential—these are the skeleton of a carpet. Test their strength by twisting the rug very gently. As a rule, if you do hear even a slight cracking sound, the warp and weft threads are probably in poor condition and the rug should be avoided.

Next, make sure that the carpet is complete. Sometimes, if a dealer has been unable to sell an awkwardly shaped or large carpet, such as a long *kenareh*, or runner, he might have this cut down into two or three smaller, and more marketable, pieces. When skilfully done, such amputations are hard to spot, but they significantly reduce the carpet's value. Look at the top and bottom fringe areas and selvedges of the carpet. They are particularly vulnerable to wear, and may become damaged while the rest of the carpet is still reasonably sound. If this happens, a restorer may chop back the damaged pieces to a suitable line of the design and refinish along the cuts. Once you own a carpet, remember to check the fringes and selvedges every few years to see if they need any repairs. If they do, it is better to have this done right away or you risk losing some of the carpet in restoration.

Now look for any areas which have been repaired or repiled. An accomplished repair is almost impossible to see, but even the very best feel slightly different from original areas of the carpet. Holding the carpet between the flats of your hands—one above, one below—slide your hands slowly from side to side. You should be able to feel a slight roughness or thickening in areas which have been repaired. Don't be disappointed if you do find one or two small repairs. As long as they are well done they make only a slight difference to the value of the carpet. However, if there are a large number of repairs, or if the quality of those repairs is substandard, the carpet is probably not a worthwhile purchase.

As well as checking those areas which have been repaired, look for any which might still need repairing. Ask for the carpet to be held up to a window or other light source while you check for small holes and areas that have worn thin. Once again, the discovery of one or two small areas in need of repair should not cause concern. Simply ask the dealer to carry out the repairs before you complete payment for your purchase.

Always avoid carpets which have been "painted"—this technique is not so much a repair as a cosmetic cover-up. When areas of pile begin to wear thin, the foundation threads show through. To conceal this defect, both the foundation and any remaining pile may be painted with dye. Although a casual observer may not notice that a carpet has been painted, this is one check which even absolute beginners can spot quite easily if they take the trouble to look carefully. Painted carpets are often disposed of at auctions, where bidders have neither the time to examine the lots nor the knowledge to notice the problem.

It does not really matter if a carpet is dirty. A certain amount of grime builds up over years of use and can be removed by a specialist carpet cleaner. Heavy soiling, however, can conceal permanent stains that would drastically reduce the value of a piece. If you are considering buying a carpet that looks very dirty, ask the dealer to have part of it cleaned before you make your final decision.

What to pay

Reproductions masquerading as the real thing, new rugs given an artificial patina of age and an artificially high price to match, mercerized cotton carpets sold as silk—all these can confuse the beginner. Only when you are confident that your chosen carpet is what it says it is, and that it is complete and in good condition, are you ready to discuss price.

This is not to say, however, that all carpets from the same area of a particular size, design and colour are automatically worth the same amount. At a certain level, the skill of the weaver can have a dramatic influence on price. This "star quality" is hard for the novice to spot, but may help to explain a difference in the prices of two apparently similar pieces.

By the time you make a purchase you will have looked through enough carpets to have a reasonably good idea about current market prices. It is useful to know how that price has been reached. There are six basic elements that determine the price of a carpet: the quality of the raw materials; the skill of the artist and time he or she spends on the piece; the quality of the weaving; the city, village or tribe that the carpet comes from; the condition of the piece; and its colour and design.

Traditionally, material costs and weavers' profit have been extremely low. Tribal and village carpets were made using wool from the weaver's own sheep and coloured with natural dye stuffs gathered from the wild, so incurring little or no costs. In addition, the concept of time as a marketable commodity was largely alien in the weaving countries of the East. Money simply did not enter the equation until the time came to sell a carpet, often after many years of use in the weaver's home. As a result, the final price was often ridiculously low by any Western standard of market value.

Only in this way could a finely crafted item, which had taken months or possibly years to complete, still have a price tag of just three or four figures. Even carpets from city workshops, where the weavers have always been paid by the day, have been unrealistically cheap by any standards.

This state of affairs could continue only as long as the populations of the weaving nations were happy to live in the traditional way at largely subsistence levels—and while the cost of living in those countries remained low. In recent years, however, the situation has begun to change. Increasing industrialization has lured more and more weavers away from their looms and into the factories. Meanwhile, the cost of living has begun to rise and those who remain true to their craft need ever higher wages simply to maintain the same standard of living.

The effects of these changes are not having an immediate impact on the Western market because it takes years for a carpet to find its way from the weaver's loom to a shop. But the impact will most certainly come in time. Prices will rise and they will continue to rise. This trend will be exacerbated by the fact that even though there are far fewer weavers now than ever before, it still takes the same amount of time to produce a fine oriental carpet. And if some weavers drop their standards to increase their output, the value of those carpets still produced with traditional care and attention will rise yet higher still.

Despite all of these factors, the prices of Persian carpets are surprisingly reasonable at the time of writing. Since the revolution of 1979 the Iranian economy has stagnated. A combination of a massive inflation rate and the Iraq/Iran war has caused the Iranian currency to drop dramatically in value against the dollar and other leading currencies. Before the revolution, there were seven tomans to the U.S. dollar and eleven tomans to one pound sterling. At the time of writing, there are 440 tomans to the dollar and 700 tomans to the pound. This exchange rate means that the prices of Persian carpets seem remarkably low for such great works of art.

But matters could change. Fifty years ago, amateur enthusiasts could buy carpets by the bale. Today, fine carpets are already beyond the reach of ordinary pockets. Even more serious are the effects of the continuous rise of industrialization in the East. Hand-crafted works of art, including hand-knotted carpets, which take time and great expertise to create, are becoming increasingly rare. It is possible that within a generation the great tradition of carpet weaving will become a thing of the past.

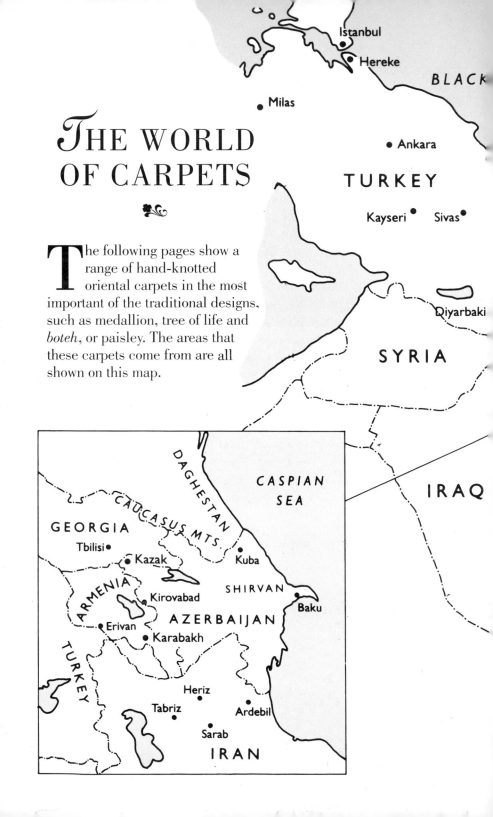

THE WORLD OF CARPETS

The following pages show a range of hand-knotted oriental carpets in the most important of the traditional designs, such as medallion, tree of life and *boteh*, or paisley. The areas that these carpets come from are all shown on this map.

Istanbul

Hereke

BLACK

Milas

Ankara

TURKEY

Kayseri   Sivas

Diyarbaki

SYRIA

IRAQ

DAGHESTAN

CASPIAN SEA

CAUCASUS MTS.

GEORGIA

Tbilisi

Kazak

Kuba

ARMENIA

SHIRVAN

Kirovabad

Baku

AZERBAIJAN

Erivan

TURKEY

Karabakh

Heriz

Tabriz

Ardebil

Sarab

IRAN

Persian Tabriz

✿

387 x 300 cm (152 x 118 in)
Wool on cotton

1950s

The medallion is perhaps the most famous of oriental carpet designs. It may take the form of a diamond or sometimes a more flowerlike circular motif, placed in the centre of the ground. Usually, a quarter of the central medallion is repeated in each of the four corners. The particular design of this piece is famous throughout the world of oriental carpets. It is called the Ardebil or "sheik safi" design, after the famous early sixteenth-century carpet currently housed in London's Victoria & Albert Museum.

The principal motif here is a round medallion, surrounded by sixteen small elipses, with elongated motifs at top and bottom. Around the medallion the ground is patterned with flowers and curving arabesques. The corner pieces resemble quarter sections of the main medallion. The border is a combination of both floral and rectangular shapes contained within a pair of narrow bands. The dominant colour is muted gold, with touches of red, olive and light brown.

Persian Tabriz

🦗

305 x 200 cm (120 x 79 in)
Wool on cotton

1960s

This is a typical *mahi*, or fish, design from Tabriz. The third largest city in Iran, Tabriz is renowned for its fine rugs and a weaving tradition which stretches back centuries.

The carpet has a large diamond-shaped medallion in soft yellow surrounding another smaller medallion in a similar shape. The main ground is filled with rows of intricate floral motifs in white on dark brown. The corner pieces are in a slightly softer shade of brown. A beautiful all-over floral pattern from which white flowers shine out decorates the border. Throughout the piece, touches of olive green and soft pink give extra warmth to the dominating shades of brown, and the whole demonstrates a great harmony between colour and design.

The *mahi* design is one of the few traditional Tabriz designs. Although a version of the *herati* design, the *mahi* is now regarded as an independent motif in its own right. It may be used as an all-over pattern, though it is usually combined with a medallion design as here. The colours vary but they usually have the same soft feel that is such an attractive feature of this carpet.

••••

Turkish Hereke

❦

129 x 87 cm (51 x 34 in)
Silk on silk

1960s

This is a typical medallion design carpet from Hereke, a Turkish weaving town known for its superfine silk rugs.

The principal motif is a central eight-hooked medallion, which looks rather like a star, containing two smaller medallions. Around this central medallion design the ground is filled with a combination of floral and bird motifs. The border is composed of two bands of equal width. The inner band is filled with flower and animal motifs while the outer features flying birds and a repeat floral pattern.
The three main colours are light terracotta-pink, olive and light brown, all on a muted beige. The border echoes the colours of the main ground.

Old Herekes are valuable and are generally in private collections. The Hereke weaving industry is still active, and produces high quality carpets. In addition to the medallion design, paisley, tree of life, *mihrab* and vase designs are featured. The most common size is 152 x 100 cm (60 x 39 in), but carpets of 213 x 152 cm (84 x 60 in) and 305 x 213 cm (120 x 84 in) are also made. The material is usually silk on silk. Wool on cotton carpets are occasionally produced but cannot be compared with the silk pieces for quality.

Persian Heriz

305 x 213 cm (120 x 84 in)
Wool on cotton

Around 1900

A beautiful example of the weaving of Heriz, a town in
northern Iran. The main motif is a central medallion, typical of
Heriz carpets. Orange and navy are the dominant colours, with
touches of beige, green and medium blue. Much of the
background is muted red, with corner pieces of beige
Between the corner pieces are semi-floral motifs similar in
design to the central medallion. The border features an
all-over floral pattern on a background of dark muted indigo.
The colours are mostly of vegetable origin.

The rug is typical of Heriz weaving—coarser pieces tend to be
more geometrical in design. Heriz carpets are extremely
decorative and durable. They are highly regarded in the West
for their beauty, which increases as the colours become muted
with the passage of time.

Persian Malayer

🌿

180 x 136 cm (71 x 54 in)
Wool on cotton

Early twentieth century

Malayers are rightly famed for their quality and colour as well as an intricacy of design unusual in village carpets.

The striking design of this piece is dominated by a large central medallion, containing a cluster of red roses. These roses are drawn in an almost Expressionist style, which distinguishes them from the more precise lines of a *gol farangi* design. The corner pieces echo the central rose motifs. The border is an all-over pattern on soft blue, which, like the red inner and outer bands, picks up the colours of the central motifs. The colours are all vegetable dyes and have a striking balance and harmony.

Malayers use a number of designs, mainly *herati* and paisley, as well as the medallion motif. A soft muted terracotta is a characteristic colour of Malayers, although other colours are also used.

Turkish Kayseri

213 x 138 cm (84 x 54 in)
Silk on silk

1960s

Kayseri in central Turkey is renowned for both its silk and woollen carpets. This medallion silk is a typical piece. The main medallion is in the shape of a diamond, containing an unusual floral motif in beige with four obvious corners, and is finished top and bottom with small end motifs. The ground is filled with an all-over floral pattern and the corner pieces are large enough to meet along the two short edges. As a rule, integrated corners such as these are found only on densely patterned grounds. In carpet designs with a plain ground, the corners are usually quite separate and distinct from each other. The main border is also in a dense all-over floral pattern.

The dominant colour in this carpet is soft pastel gold on a muted beige ground. This colour scheme is common in Kayseri carpets and indeed in most modern Turkish products woven for export. The balance of colour in this carpet is exquisite, demonstrating the skill of the weaver.

Sizes are typically 305 x 213 cm (120 x 84 in) for woollen carpets and 213 x 152 cm ((84 x 60 in) for silk ones. Larger silk carpets of 600 x 400 cm (236 x 157 in) are woven to order in Kayseri.

Persian Kashan

200 x 132 cm (79 x 52 in)
Wool on cotton

1930s

The all-over geometric floral pattern of this interesting
Kashan rug is made up of a number of diamond shapes.
Each diamond contains a motif of its own and the
design builds up into a patchwork effect of soft red,
navy, light pink and muted gold. The central medallion is
outlined with a gold zig-zag line.

The corner pieces and borders feature repeat patterns of
squares containing floral and geometric motifs and echo both
the colour and design of the main field. The extreme symmetry
and precision of this carpet testifies both to the fineness of the
weave and to the skill of the weaver.

Caucasian Kazak

216 x 152 cm (85 x 60 in)
Wool on wool

Early twentieth century

This Kazak carpet has a traditional geometric medallion pattern. The central medallion, in medium blue with touches of soft red and gold, is contained within a larger medallion in the same soft red. The main ground is dark navy blue, which throws the design into sharp relief. This background also highlights the unusual corner motifs.

The four border stripes are arranged as alternating pairs, decorated with two different simple geometric designs in soft shades of blue and red and highlighted with touches of cream. These borders combine to create a pleasingly rich effect that complements the design of the main field.

Turkish Milas

🌼

335 x 244 cm (132 x 96 in)
Wool on wool

1970s

This piece is typical of the weaving from the villages around
Milas, a city in the west of Turkey. Designs vary, but these
carpets are characteristically simple and geometric. Generally,
just two or three main colours are employed, usually red, beige
and blue. The most common motif is the central medallion, as
in this example, and occasionally the medallion is repeated to
form an all-over pattern.

In this carpet, the border design is a repeat diamond-shaped
medallion with a strong red and white colouring, which is
kept from being overpowering by thin inner and outer bands in
pale blue. Thematically, the design of this carpet owes its
origins to Persian Heriz carpets, which are simple but
beautiful. Their designs are among the most popular in the
world of oriental carpets.

This type of Turkish carpet is fairly durable and usually less
expensive than those made in Ushak, Hereke, Kayseri, Kars
and Sivas. Sizes range from 183 x 122 cm (72 x 48 in) up to
very large pieces of 610 x 488 cm (240 x192 in). Occasionally,
square carpets measuring 213 x 213 cm (84 x 84 in) are made.
Vegetable dyes are still used and consequently the abrash seen
in this carpet is not unusual.

Persian Bakhtiari

🌸

213 x 152 cm (84 x 60 in)
Wool on cotton

1950s

This rug was woven by the Bakhtiaris, tribes who live in the
Zagros Mountains in the west of Iran, and is a particularly
fine example of their craft. The carpet is decorated with the *gol
farangi* design, which comprises a number of large red roses in
the centre of the carpet on a cream background. The whole
motif is surrounded by a diamond-shaped medallion. The
geometric floral border is interesting and more typical of those
found on the city rugs of Tabriz or some parts of Isfahan than on
tribal rugs such as this.

The dominant colour is muted madder red, with muted dark
navy and a strongly contrasting cream that lifts the central
design and the border motifs. All the colours are vegetable
dyes. Unusually for a tribal rug, the pile is wool on
cotton—most tribal rugs are woven on wool foundation threads.
Bakhtiari *gol farangi* rugs are usually about 213 x 152 cm
(84 x 60 in), but are also produced in larger sizes.

In Persia, *gol farangi* means "foreign rose", giving some clue
to the French origins of this design. Most of the Karabakh rugs
woven in the Caucasus, as well as some Bijar and Senneh rugs,
are woven in this design, but is more unusual to see a Bakhtiari
rug with this motif.

Persian Mashad

🌿

183 x 122 cm (72 x 48 in)
Wool on wool

1970s

This striking example of a modern Mashad combines the beauty of a tribal design with the accuracy and fine finish of a city weave. The design originates from the Qashqai rugs from the southwest of Iran, although it also features in some Caucasian pieces. The fine weave allows greater detail, proportion and symmetry than is possible in coarser tribal rugs.

The central motif is a diamond-shaped medallion filled with semi-floral motifs and surrounded by a contrasting muted blue. The corner pieces have an all-over pattern and are in the same beige as the central medallion. The borders feature a continuous floral pattern combined in a chainlike motif.

The strong but simple design and the use of two contrasting main colours, beige and blue, contribute to the success of this unusual and attractive carpet.

Caucasian
Shirvan

325 x 121 cm (128 x 48 in)
Wool on wool

Early twentieth century

This Shirvan illustrates a characteristic of Caucasian carpets—when using large motifs, such as the octagonal medallions here, the available space is often filled with a variety of geometrical designs. The abrash noticeable in the red and blue medallions is typical of village weavings using vegetable dyes. The lack of consistency is part of the charm of this piece.

Caucasian Shirvan

🌿

370 x 168 cm (146 x 66 in)
Wool on wool

Early twentieth century

Two geometric patterns are combined in this Shirvan carpet. An all-over *boteh*, or paisley, design is overlaid by three medallions running down the centre of the field. The medallion motif is further echoed at the corners and down the sides of the field.

Caucasian Shirvan

❧

206 x 150 cm (81 x 59 in)
Wool on wool

1920s

Shirvans are among the best known types of carpet from the Caucasus and are famous for their quality and wealth of patterns. Shirvan designs are always geometric, usually in the form of one or several rows of medallions in a striking combination of muted red and navy blue on creamy beige ground. They are similar to the rugs produced by the neighbouring Kazaks, although Shirvans are generally of a much finer weave.

Here, the three major medallions are in the centre of the rug, one in cream on a red background and the other two in medium blue on beige. At the top of the rug is an unfinished medallion, rather larger than the rest, and down either side are a number of half medallions broken into the inner border. Unlike city carpets, rugs of this type rarely have completely symmetrical designs.

The border in this particular rug features a geometric all-over pattern in shades of muted red and navy on soft beige. These delightful colours have all been produced from vegetable dyes. Both pile and foundation threads are wool.

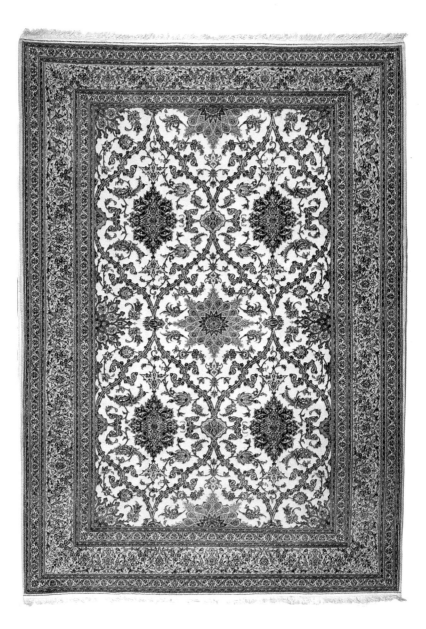

Persian Nain

305 x 213 cm (120 x 84 in)
Silk and wool on fine cotton

Mid 1960s

A typical piece from Nain in central Iran, where the weavers are renowned for making fine carpets in light colours, mainly blue and beige. The design in this particular carpet is of a rather small central medallion surrounded by four darker medallions, with half and quarter medallions carrying the design into the border. The traditional floral pattern of the border is in shades of light blue and camel on muted beige, all colours typical of Nain carpets.

Traditionally, the people of Nain made fine quality fabrics that were bought by royalty and the wealthiest nobles for their traditional robes. After the war, however, with the increasing popularity of Western-style dress, there was no longer a market for these sumptuous materials and the weavers turned to making carpets. With their history of fine fabric weaving, the first Nain carpet weavers naturally chose to produce extremely fine carpets, and that tradition continues. Remember, however, that the quality of Nain carpets does vary.

Carpets are usually in silk and wool on cotton, though there are also silk and wool on silk and pure silk pieces. The most common sizes are 213 x 152 cm (84 x 60 in) and 305 x 213 cm (120 x 84 in) but very large pieces of 610 x 396 cm (240 x 156 in) are also made.

Persian Mahal

305 x 244 cm (120 x 96 inches)
Wool on cotton

1900s

This is a beautiful example of the finest Mahal carpets known
as Zielger Mahals. These were woven in the second half of the
nineteenth century until the early twentieth century and are
highly regarded in the West for their quality and beauty.

The design is a combination of a rare type of medallion and an
all-over floral pattern. The most striking features are the four
main medallions in green and beige. In the centre of the carpet
are three smaller medallions, with two pairs of half medallions
breaking into the inner borders. The rest of the field is filled
with leaf motifs and floral patterns in a combination of
terracotta and beige on a navy ground. The border is an
all-over floral pattern in navy and green on muted terracotta.

This piece is signed and dated. The inscription reads as
follows, 1333 Hijri, 1911 AD.

Persian Qashqai

❧

213 x 152 cm (84 x 60 in)
Wool on wool

1900s

This is a striking example of the fine rugs made by the Qashqai tribes of southern Iran. The harmony of its coloration and design is typical of Qashqai rugs, which are renowned for their beauty and originality.

The design features three diamond-shaped medallions, one in beige and two in red, filled with various geometric and semi-floral patterns. The main field consists of various floral and geometric motifs in beige and red on a blue background and the border has an all-over geometric pattern on a beige ground.

Fine Qashqais can be extremely valuable and many older pieces are in private collections and museums.

Persian Ardebil

🌿

188 x 135 cm (74 x 53 in)
Wool on cotton

1960s

Carpets made in Ardebil, a small town near the Caspian Sea in northern Iran, are not to be confused with the famous carpet in London's Victoria & Albert Museum. Although that carpet came from the Ardebil mosque, it was woven elsewhere, probably in Kashan as the inscription "Kashani", meaning someone from Kashan, suggests.

With its geometric designs and other elements associated with Kazak and Shirvan carpets of the Caucasus, this example is typical of carpets made in Ardebil. The Caucasian influence is seen in the S-pattern decorating the field, while the eight-pointed star at the centre of the medallion is a particular characteristic of Shirvans.

Ardebil carpets are known for their symmetrical and proportionate design, featuring straight and accurately drawn lines. Colours are striking, usually red or orange terracotta as here, and set against a beige ground.

Caucasian Shirvan

155 x 118 cm (61 x 46 in)
Wool on wool

Early twentieth century

This Shirvan carpet is unusual for its muted colouring—dark red and blue are more traditional in Shirvans. Where touches of blue do occur here, however, they are the more striking for the contrast. The navy border frames the field, while the medium blue in the lower medallion is unusual and attractive. Both the blues harmonize well with the beige, light brown and orange of the rest of the carpet. The use of wool on wool is typical of Caucasian carpets generally and of Shirvans in particular. All the colours are vegetable dyes.

The motifs used are characteristic of Caucasian carpets. The octagonal medallions are filled with crosses, while the surrounding field is busy with lesser floral, bird and animal motifs, which are all geometrical and highly stylized. The S-pattern also appears. The borders bear a repeat leaf and flower pattern in varying degrees of realism and abstraction.

Persian Tabriz

210 x 152 cm (83 x 60 in)
Silk and wool on silk

1960s

This superb piece is an example of the very best of Tabriz
weaving and is typical of the modern Persian tendency to
combine a number of traditional designs on a single rug. In this
carpet there are flowers, animals and birds, which demonstrate
the weaver's high level of skill, as well as the main tree of life
motif. (The tree of life is a popular design, religious in origin.)
Four smaller trees also feature, one in each corner. The
dominant colours are brown and pink on light camel. The
border is just as intricate as the main ground and is packed
with flowers, birds and animals in shades of light gold and
muted lilac on a soft beige ground.

Tabriz is renowned as a weaving centre. Although its
traditional designs are the *herati*, or fish, design and the *haji
jalili*, a medallion in a plain field with a floral border, it has
produced versions of almost all the traditional oriental designs
since the war. What distinguishes a Tabriz carpet is the local
style of weaving, which is always of good quality. Materials are
usually wool on cotton, wool and silk on cotton, and wool and
silk on silk. Silk on silk carpets are occasionally made.

Persian Tehran

213 x 152 cm (84 x 60 in)
Silk and wool on silk

early 1970s

This rug comes from Tehran, the capital of Iran and its largest city. The weavers of Tehran are not known for weaving great quantities of carpets, but the quality of those they do produce is superb and can match anything from the renowned weaving centres of Isfahan, Tabriz and Kashan.

This carpet is decorated with an elaborate form of the tree of life motif. At the bottom of the carpet is a small pond from which a many-branched tree rises and spreads over the whole ground. The branches of the tree are filled with a colourful variety of fruits, birds and even nests, all realistically drawn. The colours are finely balanced in soft shades of medium blue, pink, red, golden yellow and brown. The border design is in the Isfahan weaving tradition, with its repeat pattern of red roses and small trees. The colours are very similar to those of the main design, but the fawn background of the border makes the colours seem deeper here than they do against the cream of the main ground. The pale main ground creates a striking effect and is a feature more commonly found in the carpets of Isfahan. In many other parts of Iran, a red or navy blue background would be more usual.

This type of design can be seen in many other modern Persian city rugs, in particular those of Isfahan, Qum and Tabriz.

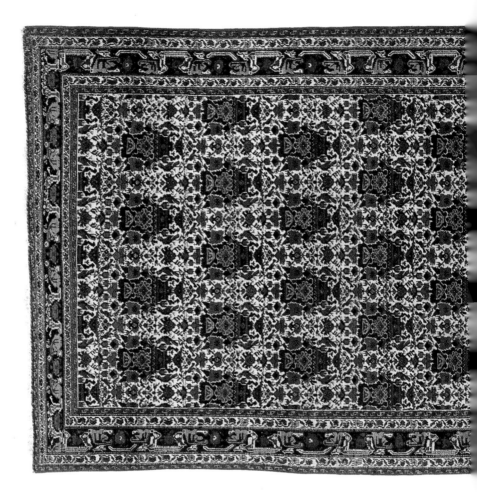

Persian Abadeh

🦋

202 x 150 cm (80 x 59 in)
Wool on cotton

1920s

All-over is a term used for any carpet where the entire ground is filled with a systematic repetition of a single motif. This piece is a typical example of an all-over *zeli-soltan* design. This particular motif is one of the most original and recognizable Persian motifs. It comprises a bunch of large red roses, either in a small vase or alone. The proportion of vase to flowers, the size of the motif and the colours it is worked in may all vary, but essentially the design remains the same. The *zeli-soltan* originated in the Hamadan area, but since the turn of the century it has spread throughout Iran to many weaving centres, including Abadeh. It has not really been adopted by weavers outside Iran, however.

In this fine carpet, the *zeli-soltan* is worked in red and blue on a mainly beige background. The spaces in between have been filled with much smaller all-over floral motifs, also in red and blue. On either side of every vase are a pair of love birds, which in Persian tradition symbolize love and marriage. The border is a fascinating combination of floral and semi-floral all-over patterns in red and muted gold on navy blue. The striking colours used in this rug are all vegetable dyes.

Persian Senneh

195 x 132 cm (77 x 52 in)
Wool on cotton

Early twentieth century

Senneh is the capital of Iranian Kurdistan and is renowned for its superfine rugs and beautiful *kilims*. This carpet, in which intricacy of design and balance of colour combine to supreme effect, is an example of Senneh weaving at its best. What at first sight appears to be an all-over floral pattern is revealed on closer inspection to be a sophisticated version of the *mina khani*, or daisy, design. The great density of decoration is perhaps rather unusual for a rug of this size. Four cheetahlike animal motifs in soft orange-pink, one in each corner, and two peacocklike birds halfway down the sides of the rug, have been added to the all-over pattern. Weaving animals and birds is a difficult task, which if badly done may ruin the artistic merit of a carpet. By including such motifs here, the weaver demonstrates his skill. The borders, filled with floral and geometric motifs, are also finely worked.

The light orange-pink and red of the roses and the dark navy blue ground are typical of Senneh colouring. The other common Senneh design of multi-medallions—a medallion within a medallion within a medallion—is also worked in these colours. Senneh rugs are woven in wool on cotton, or more rarely wool on silk. The most common size is 213 x 152 cm (84 x 60 in) although carpets measuring 305 x 213 cm (120 x 84 in) are sometimes made.

Persian Kashan

350 x 334 cm (138 x 132 in)
Silk on silk

1940s

This style of Kashan silk carpet is instantly recognized by its pale greyish colouring, not found in any other kind of oriental carpet. These so-called Grey Kashans are woven almost exclusively for the Western market.

In this particular carpet, the colours are extremely soft and well balanced, with the dominant shade of light grey set off by touches of medium blue. Although this colouring is a comparatively recent development, the design is a traditional one, basically an all-over floral pattern with six large *islimis*, or curling scrolls, arranged in pairs down the centre of the field. The border is also a traditional all-over floral pattern.

Grey Kashans are produced in pure silk on silk and in wool on cotton in a good range of sizes. The most common are 198 x 130 cm (78 x 51 in) and 305 x 198 cm (120 x 78 in), but others are available. Traditional Kashans are similar in design but tend to be coloured in a combination of madder red and deep navy blue, with touches of green, medium blue and beige.

Kashan and its surrounding area has a tradition of carpet weaving that stretches back many centuries, and some of the carpets made here are regarded as among the most durable and beautiful of all those woven in the Middle East.

Persian Veramin

245 x 130 cm (96 x 51 in)
Wool on wool

1940s

The design of this carpet is an all-over, semi-geometric, floral pattern, known as the *mina khani*, or daisy, motif. It is a very balanced and harmonious design, with flowers worked in orange, soft pink, medium blue and beige. The border has an intricate all-over geometric pattern in muted orange and medium blue on beige. Both inner and outer border stripes are in the same colours as the main background and feature all-over floral patterns.

Many modern Veramin rugs have all-over floral patterns similar to that on this piece.

Central Asian Yomut

177 x 94 cm (70 x 37 in)
Wool and silk on wool

Early twentieth century

The respect and status enjoyed by women in Turkoman society in part depended on their weaving skills. A woman's first and most important test came on her wedding day, when the bridal camel was draped with woven trappings like the one illustrated here. After the wedding, this and her other weavings, including storage bags and floor carpets, would decorate the tent where guests might be received at any time and appearances were a matter of intense pride. The fringe here shows that this trapping has been woven wider than it is deep for hanging horizontally.

Unusually for a tribal weaving, this example includes silk as well as wool. The typical dark red of Turkoman carpets is here

confined to the borders, which are remarkable for their intricate patterns. The all-over design includes hooked *gols* of an almost diamond shape, typical of the Yomut tribe, which share the field with fuller, more obviously octagonal *gols*. A pleasing abrash helps harmonize their pink colour with the brown field.

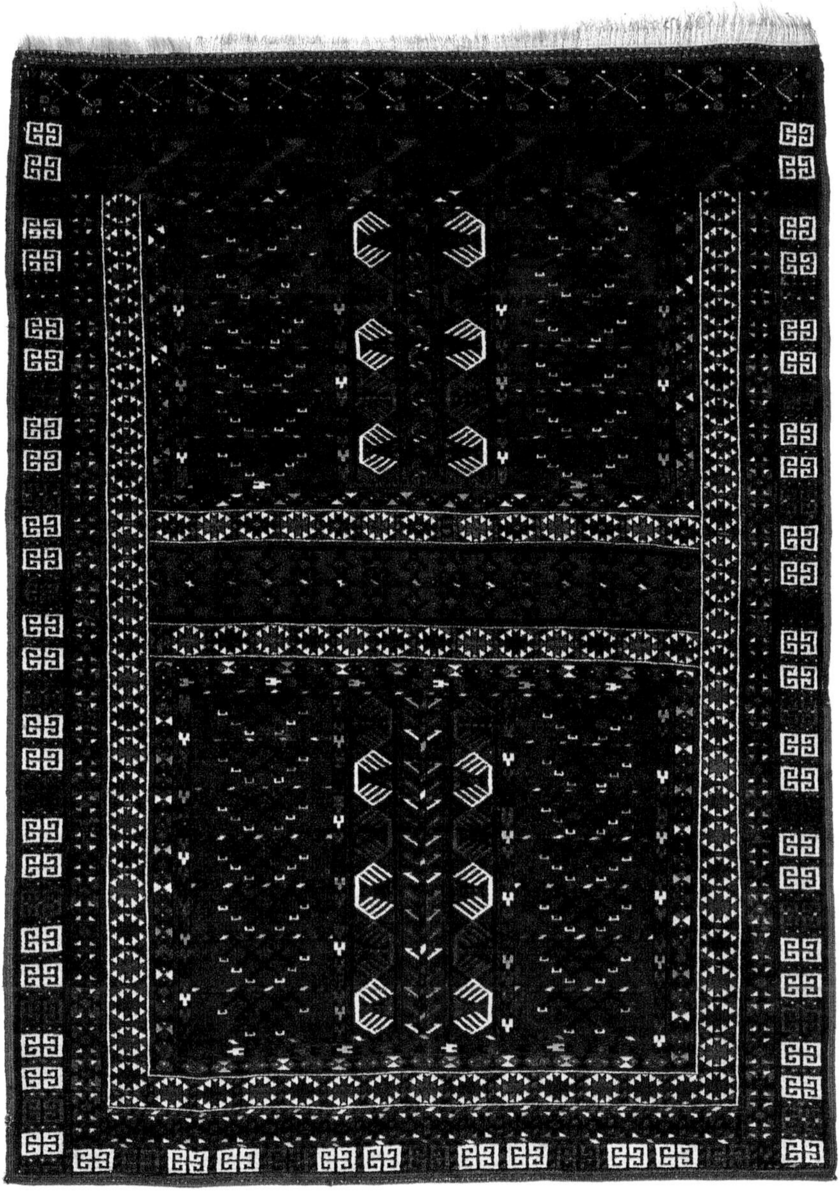

Central Asian Yomut

188 x 159 cm (74 x 63 in)
Wool on wool

1950s

The word *hatch* means cross and *hatchli* means marked with a cross. *Hatchli* is the favoured pattern for those piled carpets called *enessi*, which Turkoman tribes once hung across the entrance to their tents. Often there are two straps for this purpose at the top of the carpet.

At one time, *hatchli* carpets were assumed to have been made by Christian weavers. In fact, the design has nothing to do with the Christian cross. *Hatchlis* are found throughout Central Asia. This wonderfully intricate example is from the Yomut tribe of Turkmenistan. Delicate touches of white, yellow and various shades of blue and red enliven the overall impression of dark red. The all-over design, composed of several intersecting diagonal lines within each panel, is typical of *hatchlis* and is an elaboration of a simpler candlestick motif. The double-T pattern round the borders identifies the carpet as Turkoman work.

Central Asian Yomut

🌼

350 x 200 cm (138 x 79 in)
Wool on wool

1950s

This is a typical Yomut carpet from Turkmenistan, to the east of the Caspian Sea. The design, which is unique to Yomut rugs, is a repetition of a geometric motif made up of a number of combined swastikas. The border is filled with a repeat design in black, red and white and the rest of the carpet is coloured in white, red, orange and a dominant brownish-rust.

The use of a deep rust-brown or red is typical of most of the weaving areas in the eastern Caspian region and the dyes are all vegetable in origin. The quality of the Yomut weave ranges from a rather coarse nomadic grade to much finer versions produced in towns and even cities. The distinctive qualities of the rugs from this area are highly prized and some of the finer pieces can match the best of oriental carpets.

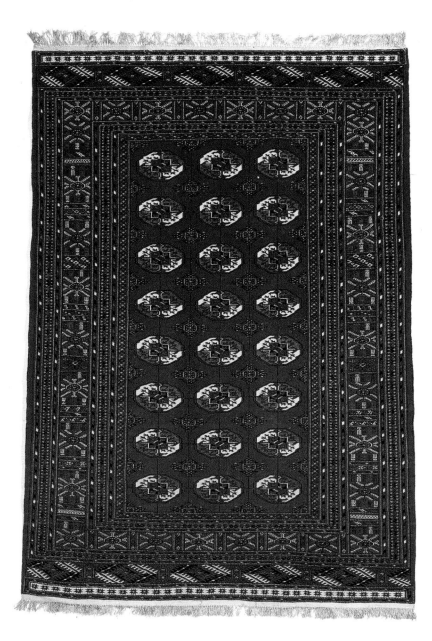

Central Asian Bukhara

🌸

211 x 155 cm (83 x 61 in)
Wool on wool

1960s

This carpet was woven in the city of Bukhara, which centuries ago was the capital of the Islamic empire.

The design of this carpet originated in Bukhara but is now one of the most common throughout the weaving countries of the East. It is particularly popular in Pakistan and India, although the quality of rugs made there is far inferior. The principal motif is the *gol*, or rose. The design is formed by a repetition of the *gol* motif in combination with a minor motif that is repeated to fill the spaces in between. The main border has an all-over geometric pattern with a smaller *gol* positioned in the centre of each motif. This main border is surrounded by a number of much narrower inner and outer border stripes in a combination of black and white knots.

The dominant colour of this carpet is a deep rich red of vegetable origin. This tendency to use one dominant colour, whether red, rust or brown, is a feature of all Bukharas and of other Central Asian rugs such as those of the Yomut, most of the Afghan tribes and the tribes of the northeast of Iran such as the Turkomans and Baluchis.

Original Bukhara carpets are highly prized if in good condition. Sizes range from 183 x 122 cm (72 x 48 in) up to 305 x 213 cm (213 x 84 in) or slightly larger.

Persian Veramin

❧

163 x 104 cm (64 x 41 in)
Wool on cotton

1960s

This is a typical *mina khani,* or daisy, design from Veramin, a town 32 kilometres (20 miles) southeast of Tehran and largely populated by Kurds and Lurs of Senneh and Bijar. Although these tribal people settled in the town centuries ago, they have continued to weave their traditional patterns and colour combinations. Thus the *mina khani* design, which originated among the Kurds, decorates many of the carpets woven in Veramin.

The *mina khani* design in this all-over carpet is made up of the repetition of a single large rose motif across the entire ground, linked with curved lines and filled out with smaller floral motifs in the spaces between. The border design here is also typical. It echoes the main floral pattern and its colours but is reduced in size to fit the narrow stripe. In some large Veramin and Kurdistan carpets with wider border stripes, the main floral motif may be copied into the border in the same size as on the main ground.

As in this example, Veramin carpets usually have a navy blue background, which offsets the roses worked in soft orange. Sometimes, however, the roses are worked in strong red.

Pakistani "Bukhara"

168 x 130 cm (66 x 51 in)
Wool on cotton

1980s

With a little experience, Pakistani rugs can be easily distinguished from most other oriental rugs by their colour range, weave, material and design. They are relatively inexpensive compared with Persian and Caucasian carpets, but may not be such good value as they first appear since they rarely have the durability or artistic merit of carpets from traditional weaving centres.

The design of this typical example has been based on the *gol* motif of the Persian Bukhara tribe. It comprises repeated pairs of *gols* in something resembling the Bukhara manner, though additional elements have been added to create a much more ornate piece than any tribal weaver would produce. This over-ornamentation detracts from the artistic qualities of the original design.

The soft pastel colours on deep red and the geometric design are both characteristic features of Pakistani rugs. The most frequently used materials are wool on cotton, silk on cotton or silk and wool on cotton.

Persian Qum

🍂

298 x 196 cm (117 x 77 in)
Silk on silk

1960s

The garden design in this unique, high quality carpet is the
traditional preserve of the Bakhtiari tribe of western Iran.
The design is characterized by a number of parallel and equal
squares, each containing a different motif. These include
animals, birds, trees, flowers, vases or almost any other
simplistic motif, geometric or floral, that the tribal weaver
might observe in daily life.

Like all tribal weavers, Bakhtiaris usually work in wool, with a
coarse knot count which forces their designs to be geometric.
In contrast, the weaving industry of Qum was established
during the 1930s and tends to concentrate on silk pieces,
which allow a fine knot count and intricately drawn designs.
Consequently, this example is a curvilinear and finer version of
the traditional tribal design. The main colours are typical of
modern Qums, basically a soft pink with a touch of turquoise
and a balanced portion of beige. The border ground is in rich
pink-red, contained within two much narrower beige stripes

The motifs used on the main ground are mostly flowers and
trees, but there are two rows of squares containing *boteh*, or
paisley, motifs on a beige ground. The paisley motif of this
Qum garden carpet replaces the cypress tree motif that
generally dominates Bakhtiari versions.

Persian Gabbeh

❧

183 x 122 cm (72 x 48 in)
Wool on wool

1960s

This fine example of a carpet woven by the Gabbeh tribes of southwestern Iran is unusual for the symmetry of its design. Generally there is no sense of balance or symmetry in gabbehs. Weavers include any design, motif or colour that they

like, using motifs of flowers, animals, birds and any other
objects found in nature. Often the colours are extremely vivid.
Here, the panel design is simplistic, composed of a
number of rows of blocks of colour from one end to the other.
The border is an all-over semi-floral pattern on a beige
background. The size of this rug is typical—gabbehs rarely
come in larger sizes. The largest made are possibly about
335 x 244 cm (132 x 96 in).

Gabbehs are much admired in the
West today for their eccentricity and originality of colour and
design. Many modern painters and textile designers have been
inspired by the beauty of these tribal pieces.

Persian Baluchi

🍀

183 x 107 cm (72 x 42 in)
Wool on wool

1950s

The Baluchis were, and some still are, a nomadic tribal people, who live along the eastern borders of Iran and into Pakistan and Afghanistan. Nomadic Baluchis produce pileless weavings, but today piled carpets in distinctive dark colours are woven by Baluchis who have settled in villages in the Khorasan region of northeast Iran. The Baluchis are known for their use of deep red, dark brown and often a strong rust colour, combined with dark blue.

In this example, the geometric floral pattern of the central field suggests two designs: the *gol* associated with Bukhara carpets of Central Asia, and the *mina khani*, or daisy, motif of Veramin. Hooked diamonds, which can be seen as stylized tarantulas, run round the main border and round that in turn is a geometric reciprocal pattern. These design elements and the small size, together with the fact that the carpet has been woven in wool on wool, show that this is a tribal weaving, not the product of a city workshop.

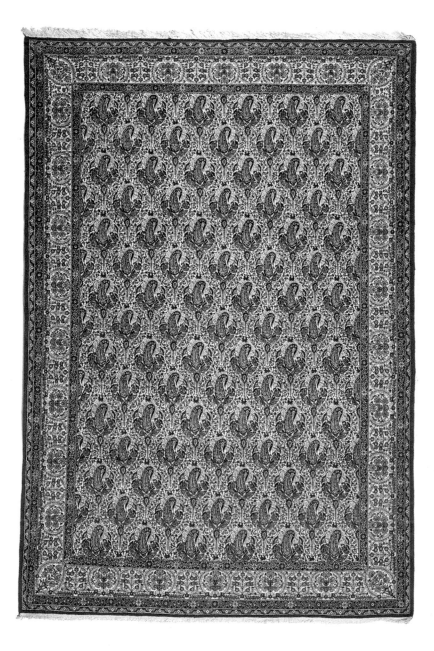

Persian Qum

335 x 222 cm (132 x 87 in)
Wool on cotton

1950s

The design of this carpet, woven in the major production centre of Qum in central Iran, is based on the *boteh*, or paisley, motif. The *boteh* is one of the most popular motifs in the East, especially in Iran. Its shape and size may vary and it may be combined with other designs or arranged in rows or repeat patterns, but it is always instantly recognizable.

This is a typical example of an all-over paisley design. The carpet has a high knot count, which means that the motif can be very finely drawn. The *botehs* are all the same size and are evenly spaced; they all face in the same direction, and they are worked in the same muted gold with touches of pink and green. This repetition creates a great sense of harmony in the piece. Strands of smaller floral motifs twine between the *botehs* to create a sort of curvilinear grid. The border is filled with an all-over floral pattern in the same muted colour range.

The softer colours used here are typical of many post-war city carpets, made to appeal to Western markets. Only in the towns and villages, which are less dependent on distant market forces, are the strong and vibrant colours traditionally favoured by Eastern weavers still used.

Turkish Hereke

305 x 213 cm (120 x 84 in)
Wool on cotton

1980s

Hereke is known for its silk rugs but this is a fine example of a woollen piece with a paisley, or *boteh*, design. The paisley design can take many different shapes and forms. Here, it comes in the form of pairs of tear-drops worked in different colours, mainly red, beige and olive, with touches of light blue. The background is completely filled with a floral motif in soft pinkish red on a deep navy background.

The border is an all-over floral pattern contained within two inner and outer bands, referred to as "guards". These are worked in the same colour combination as the paisley motifs on a striking beige background.

Caucasian Kazak

🐚

203 x 122 cm (80 x 48 in)
Wool on wool

Early twentieth century

This is an excellent example of a top-quality Kazak carpet. It is decorated with a geometric all-over paisley, or *boteh*, pattern in beige, soft pink and blue. The background is navy blue and shows noticeable abrash.

The main border is an interesting variation on the all-over geometric pattern and is coloured in shades of muted red, gold and blue on a beige ground. The smaller inner and outer borders are also attractive. The inner border is filled with a simple geometric design on a soft orange-red ground, while the outer is adorned with a very basic interlocking design in red and blue.

Persian Senneh

305 x 213 cm (120 x 84 in)
Wool on cotton

1970s

This is a superb example of weaving from Senneh, the capital of Iranian Kurdistan. It uses the *gol farangi*, or foreign flower, design, which results from the French influence on Persian carpets in the eighteenth century.

Here, the design consists of repeated bunches of roses and flowers, which occupy the whole of the main field. The red roses are very prominent and the motifs are highly symmetrical. The other colours used are medium blue and deep green on a navy background. The border features an all-over floral pattern in medium blue with touches of green on a red background. The whole design is exquisitely balanced and harmonious.

Senneh rugs are renowned for their fine weave. Some, particularly the older pieces, are so fine that the knots cannot be counted by the naked eye. Other Sennehs have larger knots, however, and knot size is not an indication of quality.

····
119

Caucasian Karabakh

🙟

244 x 152 cm (96 x 60 in)
Wool on wool

1920s

This *gol farangi* piece comes from Karabakh, one of the most famous carpet weaving centres in the whole of the Caucasus and well known for its floral rugs.

The design of this rug is made up of four bunches of roses framed by ruffs of green leaves. Down either side of the main ground are rows of much smaller roses. The four central bunches of roses resemble four major medallions laid in a row down the centre of the rug. The border is a beautiful all-over floral pattern in red and pink on a dark striking navy blue, which contrasts well with the muted red of the main background.

Most Karabakh rugs are about this size and the *gol farangi* is a typical design although the size and shape of the roses vary. The colours are mostly vegetable dyes and the materials are usually wool on wool.

Persian Qum

366 x 274 cm (144 x 108 in)
Silk on silk

1930s

The *moharamat* is a rare and original Persian design, which is composed of a number of stripes of different widths running from one end of the carpet to the other. In this striking example, there are stripes in three colours, red, black and beige, each featuring an all-over floral pattern in muted shades. The main border has an all-over floral pattern on a red background.

This exquisite carpet is remarkable for its harmony and colour balance. Like other early Qums, it has a timeless appeal which is appreciated by West and East alike.

Persian Qashqai

265 x 175 cm (104 x 69 in)
Wool on wool

1950s

Carpets of this design have traditionally been associated with the Qashqai tribal confederation of southwest Iran. The field is decorated with a pattern known as the *cane moharamat*, each of its stripes embellished with floral motifs.

Such carpets are renowned for their beautiful colours, a tradition which is evident in this example. The remarkable range of shades of brown, gold, red, orange and blue, given an additional lift by beige and white stripes, lends great intricacy to what at first glance is a deceptively simple overall pattern.

Persian Qum

🌾

224 x 142 cm (88 x 56 in)
Wool on cotton

1960s

This striking example of the popular vase design was made in the modern weaving centre of Qum. The principal motif is the vase, filled with a large blossoming tree with elegantly arching side branches. The secondary design is a beautiful prayer arch, with flower-filled corners and two all-over floral columns.

The combination of vase and prayer arch designs is a common one in both Persian and Turkish carpets, but the motifs are often placed on an intricately patterned ground which, at first glance, can almost camouflage them. In this carpet, a pale beige ground makes the richly coloured design stand out in sharp, almost startling, relief.

The border has a dense, all-over floral pattern in reddish-pink on dark navy blue with small beige flowers. The outer and inner border stripes are in a red all-over floral pattern.

Qum rugs are generally made in silk on silk. They come in a range of sizes of which 152 x 100 cm (60 x 39 in), 200 x 130 cm (79 x 51 in) and 300 x 200 cm (118 x79 in) are the most common.

Persian Kashan

213 x 152 cm (84 x 60 in)
Silk on silk

Late nineteenth century

K ashan is a city in central Iran with a carpet-weaving tradition that goes back centuries. This example of Kashan weaving is an old pictorial rug of pure silk, with human figures, a horse, buildings and a carefully drawn landscape. The border is filled with an all-over pattern that is traditional to Kashan. The colours are generally soft tones of pink and beige. Pink is common in old Kashan rugs, particularly in those made of silk. (In woollen rugs Kashan weavers tended to use tones of madder red and navy.)

In carpet terms, this piece is antique. Old Kashan silks of this type can be extremely valuable if in good condition and much more expensive than woollen Kashans of similar quality. Moreover, old-style silk Kashans are no longer woven in large enough quantities for export to the west. Silk carpets that are similar in theme and design to Kashans are now produced in some quantity in modern Qum.

Persian Gabbeh

🍇

188 x 105 cm (74 x 41 in)
Wool on wool

1960s

This is a simple pictorial gabbeh carpet. The human figure is drawn geometrically, using shades of muted brown and beige with touches of red, against an expanse of deep red, the traditionally favoured background colour. The border is an all-over triangular geometric pattern in three contrasting colours—beige, black and muted orange. The combination of the border colours is striking next to the simple plain red of the main ground.

Wool has been used throughout and the weave is coarse. The colours have been produced from vegetable dyes. In some gabbehs, the brightly contrasting colours and bold regularity of the border seen here might serve as the entire pattern of the carpet.

Persian Gabbeh

183 x 122 cm (72 x 48 in)
Wool on wool

1960s

The tribal peoples of the southwest of Persia, such as the Qashqai, Lurs and Bakhtiaris, weave rugs known as gabbehs as well as their own individual types. Gabbehs come in small sizes, usually 183 x 122 cm (72 x 48 in), and their designs are quite unlike those of any other kind of oriental carpet. They may be plain, divided into brightly coloured squares or zig zags, or pictorial and adorned with animal motifs.

This example is densely patterned compared with most

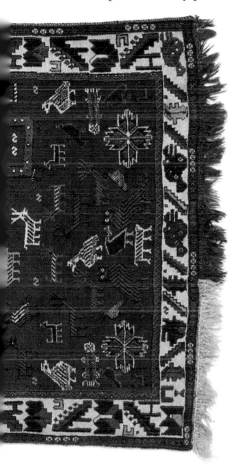

gabbehs. A large, stylized lion dominates the carpet and horses, deer, goats, cheetahs and birds crowd together around him to riotously decorative effect. The border has a semi-geometric all-over pattern, with outlandish three-legged animal motifs. This border design is worked on a lovely muted beige, but the bands on either side of it and the main ground are in a combination of vivid red and orange. Vivid colours are an important part of the gabbeh style.

Persian Qashqai

❦

265 x 175 cm (104 x 69 in)
Wool on cotton

1960s

This is a fine example of the carpet weaving skills of the
Kashkuli, a division of the Qashqai tribe who inhabit the
Fars region of southwest Iran. The Kashkuli are famous for their
elaborate patterns and fine weave.

In this example, a proliferation of delicate flowers elaborates
the core motif of a geometric vase pattern. The detail of this
mille fleurs, or thousand flowers, design can only be achieved
with a higher knot count than usual in tribal carpets, which
generally have a coarser weave. The whole design is contained
within a *mihrab*, although this is not as noticeable as usual
because of the intricacy of the design.

There is beauty, too, in the bright but harmonious use of
colour—the central yellow bounded by strong red. These
colours are contained within imaginatively patterned border
bands picked out in a rich cream.

Caucasian Kazak

🌿

178 x 91 cm (70 x 36 in)
Wool on wool

Early twentieth century

K azaks are among the most famous of Caucasian rugs and are valued for their beauty and durability. Since the production of carpets ceased in the 1920s and 30s, when this region was incorporated into the former Soviet Union, scarcity value has made these carpets still more sought after. Kazak designs are among the most original in the entire Orient. In this example, as in most of the true Kazaks, the design is geometric and the colours are vegetable-based.

The pattern consists of four pairs of diamond-shaped medallions, combined with two larger medallions in the centre of the ground, one in light brown, the other in soft pink and navy. The design is further enlivened by a number of small animal motifs and one larger one at the top of the rug. The borders are simple, consisting of two equal bands, one in brown on beige, the other in blue and soft orange.

Though the Kazak weaving industry has been largely destroyed, Kazak designs are now mass produced in Turkey. These copies, known as Turkish Kazaks, cannot match the beauty of the originals. Whereas the idiosyncrasies of the original Kazaks clearly showed that their designs evolved as the weaver worked, the Turkish Kazaks are careful copies of Kazak-style designs and display none of the imbalances and abrupt halts which are such charming features of the originals.

Central Asian Yomut

🪱

124 x 89 cm (49 x 35 in)
Wool on wool

1950s

The Yomut tribe of western Turkmenistan has been influenced by the carpet weavers of the Caucasus across the Caspian Sea. In this carpet, for example, the bold white pattern running down the three vertical stripes is similar to the ram's horn motif commonly found in Caucasian carpets. The alternating brown and black crabs running down the red stripes and on the main border are also Caucasian in inspiration.

Typically Yomut, however, is the colour range. With its rust and brown, it is less vibrantly red than the Bukhara carpets made by the Tekke tribe of eastern Turkmenistan. The carpet derives its unusual shape from the main border, which bulges outward at the top to create a prayer niche, or *mihrab*.

GLOSSARY

Abrash
Variations in tone in a single-colour area, caused by the uneven take-up of dye on handspun yarn or by the uneven fading of a colour. Abrash is most pronounced on handspun yarn that has been dyed with vegetable colours and most common in tribal rugs. The effect is highly prized by connoisseurs and consequently may sometimes be faked.

All-over design
This term is used for any carpet where the entire field is filled with a systematic repetition of a single motif (*see* pp. 86–105).

Aniline dyes
These were the earliest synthetic dyes, discovered in the mid-nineteenth century. These colours were harsh and tended to fade with time. Their drawbacks rapidly became apparent and new improved synthetic dyes were developed. Aniline dyes have not been used for many years.

Art silk
This is one name given to mercerized cotton. Mercerizing is a chemical process which can be applied to cotton thread to give it a silklike sheen. However, unlike silk, mercerized cotton does not wear well and rapidly looses its shine once walked on.

Borders
Bands, usually decorated with patterns different to that of the main field. The bands form a visual frame round the field, enhancing the main design.

Boteh
Familiar to Westerners as the paisley motif, this is one of the most common motifs in oriental carpet design (*see* p. 31 and pp. 112–117).

Cartoon
A paper pattern, usually drawn on squared paper, for the design of a carpet. Cartoons are produced by specialist designers who sell their patterns to the weavers.

Chemical washing
Also called antique washing, or antiquing. A chemical process which simulates the natural ageing process, fading colours and adding lustre to the pile. The process may cause damage and carpets which have been "washed" should generally be avoided.

Curvilinear design
The city style of carpet design which relies on a high knot count to produce intricately curved designs. Curvilinear designs are always worked from cartoons.

Double weft
A carpet is said to be double wefted when the knots which make up its pile are pulled tight asymmetrically. This technique pulls adjacent warp threads one on top of the other. This technique is most famously practiced by the weavers of Bijar.

Field
Also Ground. Both words describe the central area of a carpet, framed by the border, where the main design is worked.

GLOSSARY

•••••••••••••

Foundation
The network of warp and weft threads on to which the knots are tied. The foundations of tribal rugs are usually made of wool, giving the finished carpet a floppy feel. The foundation of city rugs and often of village rugs also, are generally cotton, which produces a firm and durable foundation. Silk may also be used.

Fringes
The trailing ends of the warp threads left, largely for decorative effect, at the top and bottom of a carpet. The fringes may be left to hang loose or be decoratively knotted according to local custom. Occasionally the fringes are worked back into the carpet out of sight. If the fringe becomes damaged, the carpet is in danger of unravelling.

Garden design
Traditionally a design of the Bakhtiari people. The field of the carpet is divided into a grid by lines which represent irrigation channels. Plant and animal motifs are placed in the squares in between (*see* pp. 106–111).

Geometric design
A design based on straight lines and sharp angles and the opposite of curvilinear. Tribal and village weavers usually make geometric designs.

Gol
Literally "flower", generally supposed to be a stylized rose. In the arid countries of the Middle East, roses are highly prized for their transient beauty (*see* p. 31).

Gol farangi
Literally "foreign flower". Based on the French Savonnerie carpets, the orientalized design is dominated by stylized, somewhat angular, cabbage roses (*see* pp. 118–121).

Herati
Also called the *mahi*, or fish, design. Basically this is a diamond enclosing a rosette, with smaller rosettes at each corner and a serrated leaf along each side. The motif has many variations (*see* p. 30).

Hunting design
Both a literal representation of a hunting scene and a reminder of heaven where hunting, the sport of kings, is one of the pastimes promised to the faithful.

Kilim
Flat-weave floor covering. There are also *kilim* ends—flat-weave bands worked at top and bottom of a carpet to secure the main piled area.

Knot count
A measure of the fineness of a carpet. The count is established by turning a carpet over and counting the number of knots within a horizontal strip of 2·5 centimetres (1 inch) and a vertical strip of 2·5 centimetres (1 inch) and then multiplying the two figures to get the count per square. Different weaving areas have different average knot counts and individual carpets should only be judged in comparison with local average knot counts (*see* p. 39).

Knot type
There are two basic knot types, each with a number of different names. The Persian knot may also be called the asymmetrical or Senneh knot. The Turkish knot is also called the symmetrical or Ghiordes knot. The names have no geographical significance, though established weaving areas do always work in either one knot or the other and the knot may therefore help to identify the origin of a particular carpet (*see* pp. 21–22).

Koran
The Islamic holy book. It is believed by Muslims to be the word of God passed on to Mohammed by the Angel Gabriel.

••••
141

GLOSSARY

•••••••••••••

Loom
The simple frame on which a carpet is worked. There are two basic types. Horizontal looms, used by nomadic weavers, are temporary structures pegged out on the ground. They can be simply rolled up for transportation,,with an unfinished carpet attached. Vertical looms are permanent structures and come in varying degrees of complexity.

Machine-made carpets
Sometimes masquerading as genuine oriental carpets, these inferior pieces are put together by machine-formed loops of pile thread (instead of knots), held in place with glue. They have no artistic merit and rapidly fall to pieces.

Medallion
This is perhaps the most famous oriental carpet design. The medallion may be a diamond or sometimes a more flowerlike circular motif, placed in the centre of the field. Usually, a quarter of the central medallion is repeated in each of the four corners of the field. The field may be patterned or plain and the medallion itself may range from simple geometric to highly elaborate curvilinear (*see* pp. 46–67).

Mihrab
Also known as the prayer arch, this typical design is particularly common in Turkish carpets. The arch recalls the architecture of the mosque and a lamp on a long chain may hang from its apex, completing the picture. The *mihrab* is often combined with the vase of immortality as a secondary design (*see* p. 32 and pp. 134–139).

Mina khani
The *mina khani* motif is made up of four flowers arranged in a diamond shape, with a smaller flower placed in the centre of the diamond. This motif is usually repeated to form an all-over design and is particularly popular with the weavers of Veramin.

Painting/Tinting
This is the practice of painting in the design on worn areas of a carpet to disguise their lack of pile, a technique which only tricks a casual observer. Painted carpets are sometimes sold at auction houses where there is less time for detailed inspection.

Palmette
A traditional motif which is thought to represent the opium poppy (*see* p. 31).

Side cords
The long edges of a carpet, side cords are often reinforced. Damage to side cords is serious and should be repaired immediately.

Tree of life
A popular design, religious in origin. The tree of life may be combined as a secondary motif with the *mihrab* (*see* p. 33 and pp. 82–85).

Vase of immortality
A popular carpet design, this features a vase which is usually shaped like a Greek urn and filled with flowers. It may be used as the main design of a carpet or repeated to form an all-over design. Tradition has imbued it with a certain religious significance. Repeated vase motifs also form part of the *zeli-soltan* design (*see* p. 33 and pp. 126–127).

Warp
The vertical threads which form part of the foundation of a carpet.

Weft
The horizontal threads which form part of the foundation of a carpet.

Zar
A traditional measure of one arm's length, which equals 100 cm (39 in). Many of the names for carpet sizes include the word *zar*—*dozar* means two *zars*, *zaronim* is one and a half *zars* (*see* p. 25).

INDEX

❧